KILLER
GENIUS

The Bizarre Case of the Homicidal Scholar

C.J. MARCH

SLINGSHOT
BOOKS

Binghamton, NY, 1870

1

The August sun was just rising over the Chenango River as the man crossed the bridge. He stopped in his tracks. Something was floating in the low water below him. The man was compelled to investigate; he was on high alert, as the rest of the town of Binghamton was, after what had just happened.

A night or two before, an eighteen-year-old guard had been at work at the Halbert Brothers dry goods store, minding the stock through the small hours. It was an important job, protecting valuable silks, among other things. Young Frederick Merrick took his responsibility seriously.

Merrick and his colleague Gilbert Burrows were sleeping in their cots at the back of the store when they were awakened by the noises of an attempted robbery. Both men tried their best to save the stock under their care, but the thieves were vicious. Burrows was stunned by a thrown chisel, and Merrick was rammed with a stool. They fought back, one of them pinning a thief against the shop counter and wringing his testicles. At first, this was as far as the scuffle went, but within minutes, Frederick Merrick had been shot in the head and killed.

The local man crossing the bridge clambered down the bank to get a better look at the strange object in the water, making his way to the shallow part of the river in which it was lying. The "thing" was a man, fully clothed and facedown, drowned. The body was pulled in by boat, and soon after, further upstream, another man noticed a second unusual, lumpy object in the water. He thought a log had gotten caught in the shallows; his wife thought it was a drowned dog.

On his way to the grocery store, he heard that a body had been found and realized the object he'd seen was neither a log nor a dog. As this second corpse was pulled in, a fishhook caught it in the eye, gouging out the eyeball. Onlookers were elated, though, both at the grizzly post-mortem blinding and at the discovery of the bodies. These were the thieves who'd killed Frederick Merrick. Divine justice had been served, even if it wouldn't bring back the murdered guard.

A newspaper illustration of the "Drowned Burglars"

Divine the justice may have been, but it was also incomplete. There had been *three* thieves that night. Running toward the store as the alarm sounded, some townspeople saw a man walking away from the commotion, out of town. One of them asked him if he knew where the fire was. "At Halberts store," said Edward Rulloff.

New Brunswick was a booming port of arrival for many immigrants from Northern Europe. In 1785, Saint John became the first incorporated city in Canada, and the province only expanded. In nearby Hammond River, Edward H. Rulloffson was born to his third-generation North American Dutch parents, William and Priscilla, in 1821. When Edward was five, his father died, leaving little to Priscilla and their three sons. Edward remembered his mother as "a Christian woman of remarkable force of character, and considerable education."

As a boy, there didn't seem to be anything unusual about Edward, though he preferred indoor activities to outdoor, read voraciously, and was obviously bright. At the end of his life, Rulloff claimed his teachers at the academy in Saint John graduated him at sixteen because he'd learned all they could teach him. Certificate in hand, but without the means to carry on his education, he took a job clerking at Keator and Thorne, a local dry goods store.

Edward was proud of his intelligence. Now living a more urban life, he also fell in with a group of young men described as "scoffers and unbelievers." Still, he'd impressed his merchant employers as studious and reliable. When the store caught on fire, the owners suspected arson, but no one connected it with their young clerk. But in Edward, it might have ignited a lifelong criminal appetite.

After the shop burned a second time, Rulloffson quit and went to work for Duncan Robertson, a local lawyer. He learned enough law to serve him later when he turned to defending himself and his collaborators in crime. Keator and Thorne, meanwhile, had set up shop again, moving into the very building on Prince Street where Robertson had his law offices. They were robbed several times, specifically in one case, of suit material. When their former clerk showed up at the building one day wearing a brand-new tailored suit made from the very cloth that had been stolen, Mr. Thorne confronted him. Far from being repentant, Rulloffson was outraged at the accusation. His family spread nasty rumors about the merchant, but Thorne pressed charges. Edward Rulloffson was tried and sentenced to his first stint in prison—two years in St. John's penitentiary, still considered one of the most dangerous prisons in Canada.

Edward Rulloffson's first stretch behind bars remains largely mysterious, but he'd set the pattern: he had no problem committing crime, including against someone he knew personally. But whatever happened in those two years behind bars, when he walked out of St. John's penitentiary, he had a new name, Edward Rulloff, and was about to graduate from theft to murder.

2

William Schutt would be sorry he ever laid eyes on the stranger he picked up in May of 1842. He was working his passenger boat around Syracuse when he met a teacher, looking for a place to start a school. The man was broke, so William agreed to let him earn his passage. His new crewman was friendly and a good worker, who even jumped into the canal to clear snags. William was increasingly impressed with his new friend's accomplishments. Edward Rulloff was someone William would be proud to invite home to Dryden with him.

Rulloff didn't tell Schutt that he had been in prison. After release, Rulloff left Canada, making his way to New York City, and stopped briefly with his brother Ruloff Rulloffson in Maine, who was building his fortune in logging. Once in the city, Rulloff took courses in bookkeeping and penmanship (a prized skill at the time) from a commercial school. He claimed the school's owner, Mr. Gourand bilked him out of money. He called the man "a humbug and a fraud."

As a guest of the well-respected Schutt family, Rulloff gained entry into Dryden's close-knit, well-ordered society of farmers and industry. They believed the well-edited story he told about himself. He worked first for a pharmacist, acquiring an extensive knowledge of drugs. When he then took a position as a schoolteacher, it was not at the free *common school*, but at the *select school*, where parents paid to

5

send their children, presumably for a better education. Among his students in the fall of 1842 and the winter of 1843 were William Schutt's sisters, Jane and Harriet.

Harriet had long dark hair and delicate features. Rulloff pursued her; to a young provincial, her teacher must have seemed the height of learning and polish. He had the knack for appearing charming and accomplished. But not everyone trusted him. When Harriet's brother Ephraim wanted proof of who he was and where he came from, Rulloff was insulted.

Despite her family's reservations, Harriet married Rulloff on New Year's Eve, 1843. Not twenty-four hours passed before his volatility erupted. William Schutt married the very next day, and the family celebrated the weddings together. At the end of the second marriage ceremony, the minister kissed both brides. Rulloff was furious. If he were a woman, he said, he "would murder a minister before he would permit him to kiss her."

By the time of the marriage, Rulloff had left his teaching job to study medicine with Dr. Stone in nearby Ithaca. Stone was a "botanical doctor," an old-school practitioner of herbal medicine. A more forward-looking practice would use modern chemistry. Rulloff knew about both approaches, evidenced by a copy on his shelf of Hooper's *Lexicon-Medicum*, a reference listing both herbal and chemical preparations. But Harriet had a cousin, a Dr. Bull, who actually practiced the modern method. It wasn't his practice of medicine, though, that bothered Rulloff. It was the kissing.

Whenever Dr. Bull visited the Schutt farm, where Rulloff and Harriet were living after their marriage, he made it his business to kiss the young Schutt sisters. He visited a lot. The Schutts ignored Rulloff's demands to stop him. Bull was family. Rulloff made Harriet cry with his jealous raging. And one day, when Rulloff didn't like the way she was crushing peppercorns in a mortar, he grabbed the pestle out of Harriet's hand and struck her on the forehead. He claimed he was only being playful. The bruise lasted days.

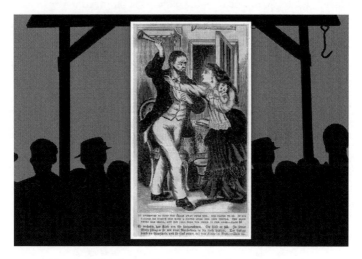

Newspaper illustration of Rulloff assaulting his wife with a pestle

By the next summer, Rulloff was convinced Harriet and Bull were lovers. He insisted his wife move with him to Ithaca. It didn't help. His resentment of her family and his obsession with Bull were now compounded by tougher financial circumstances away from the family farm. Hearing muffled cries, their new landlord, Jane O'Brien, and the woman who owned the tailor shop downstairs, Harriet Ackerman, found Harriet Rulloff holding a pillow in front of her face to protect her from Rulloff's poisoning her and then himself.

Rulloff yelled, "By the living God, this poison will kill both of us in five minutes." The women wrestled with him, and he threw the vial out the window. He accused Harriet again of an affair with Bull.

On her knees, Harriet pleaded, "Oh, Edward, I am innocent as an unborn child."

In his rage, he struck her and said to go live with Bull. That night he took Harriet back to her family and left her there. Rulloff told her sister Jane, "he sometimes felt like destroying the whole family, and then being hung like an honest man, as Clark was." Guy C. Clark had murdered his wife with an ax. Rulloff called him a gentleman. Harriet's family and friends were horrified. Still, the couple were apart now, and Harriet's father had told Rulloff never to come back. Harriet was safe.

Then she found out she was pregnant.

Rulloff and Harriet reunited. A baby needed a father, even a dangerous one. There was no love lost between him and her family. He believed they looked down on him, and it enraged him when he was "their superior in every way." He called them an "ignorant, ordinary sort of family." He pressured Harriet to move to Ohio, both to escape the family and to seek the opportunities he was sure lay west. She refused. Lansing, a hamlet on the east side of Cayuga Lake, barely five miles from her family in Ithaca, was as far as Harriet would go with him. There, Harriet gave birth on the night of April 12 to their daughter. They named her Priscilla, after his mother.

Rulloff had been a store clerk, a lawyer, then claimed to be a teacher, and now, in their new town, he set himself up as a practicing physician. Even given his lack of university training, he was not very differently educated from many who called themselves doctors at the time. Physicians were always needed, and diplomas were given out with little practical training. In Europe, the theories of Pasteur and others would lead to huge advances in the understanding of germs, but most in the American medical establishment still believed in the *miasma* theory of disease (that illness was caused by clouds of unhealthy vapors) and that ingesting certain heavy metals could cure illness.

Rulloff was undoubtedly a danger as a doctor, but so was

almost any other physician who could have been called upon in upstate New York in 1845. Rulloff's menace, however, went far beyond the standard limitations of nineteenth-century medicine.

When William Schutt's wife, Amelia, and their infant daughter, Amille, fell ill, he didn't call on their cousin, Dr. Bull, or the physician who been at Amille's birth—Dr. Oliver W. Bonney. He called Rulloff. For the second time in his association with the man, Schutt made a choice that would cost him dearly.

William's wife and baby daughter died in convulsions. But not before Rulloff had complained to Hannah Schutt, Harriet and William's mother, that William had ill-used him by letting Dr. Bull hang around. If Amelia and the baby died, he told her, they'd have William to thank for it. He mused on how strange it was that Hannah had raised all her children to adulthood without losing any, predicting that her "gray hairs would go down in sorrow to the grave."

"Who will go next?" he asked her.

Rulloff and Harriet attended both funerals, and he appeared "without outward manifestation of any consciousness of agency in their untimely end." Women and babies died all the time in those days.

○—○—○

To the Schutts and to the Rulloff's neighbors, the months he and Harriet spent in Lansing seemed peaceful. He appeared kinder; she didn't complain of ill-usage. She was happy with motherhood, and he seemed to be getting "forehanded with the world." He had his medical practice and a library, and he was studying Latin and Greek with a scholar in Ithaca. All seemed well. It couldn't last.

One day in June of 1845, when baby Priscilla was only three months old, Rulloff invited Olive Robertson, a neighbor's daughter, to come and keep Harriet company. He had to go out, and there were, he said, "Indians" in the neighborhood. He didn't want his wife to be frightened on her own.

The villages of the Cayuga tribe once lined the shores of Cayuga Lake, until the Revolutionary War and its aftermath of ethnic cleansing and unfair treaties thinned and scattered the Cayuga people. When Rulloff and Harriet lived in Lansing, the region was only a few decades from its Colonial frontier past.

Given his apparent concern about the "Indians" and Harriet's safety, the women were unsettled when he returned with two "squaws." He seemed anxious to teach Harriet and Olive about them. It was strange enough that Olive Robertson remembered the incident years later, but once the native women were gone, things got stranger.

Rulloff mixed up some medicine in a mortar and tried to give it to baby Priscilla, claiming she was ill. Harriet blocked him: whatever it was, he would not give it to her child. He told Harriet to drink it herself then. Inexplicably, she agreed. Before she could swallow it, Rulloff snatched it out of her hands and threw it in the fire. He claimed the whole thing had been a joke.

After an unnerving afternoon of "squaws" and "jokes," Olive Robertson went home. It was the last time anyone saw Harriet and Priscilla Rulloff alive.

The sun rose and the morning wore on in the town of Lansing, but the curtains of the doctor's house remained closed. It was June 24, the day after Rulloff's medicine "joke" and just a few weeks after the deaths of Schutt's wife and daughter. The curiosity of the neighbors was relieved when, in the late morning, Rulloff emerged. He went immediately to the Robertson's house across the way and borrowed a horse and wagon. His wife's uncle, he told Tom Robertson, had visited last night. The uncle had taken Rulloff's wife and child home with him to Motts Corner ten miles away for a holiday, but in order for the two to ride comfortably, the uncle had been forced to leave behind a large wooden chest that Rulloff himself would now have to transport.

Tom Robertson, Olive's father, was reluctant to loan his horse for such a long trip on a hot day, but he knew Rulloff not just as a neighbor and family man but as one of the town's doctors. He and his son helped Rulloff heave the chest into the back of the cart. Without suspicion, Robertson returned to his own home, and Rulloff drove away. He whistled and sang with a bunch of children he picked up along the way perched on the box.

He didn't go to Motts Corner, and Harriet's uncle, Henry Snyder, hadn't visited or left a chest behind. Some say Rulloff headed to Ithaca and enjoyed dinner at an inn before driving to Cayuga Lake, loading the chest in a boat and dumping the weighted bodies of Harriet and Priscilla into the water. Others swear that the victims never made it into the lake and instead, were sold for dissection to the Geneva Medical College. Two bodies of the general description of the victims arrived at the college that summer. The adult female had "long and beautiful black hair."

It was as if Rulloff was playing games with the Schutts. On his way back with Tom Robertson's cart and horse, Rulloff stopped at William Schutt's house in Ithaca and had something to eat. As Jane Schutt recounted it, he "would not wait for me to get him something to eat, but went down to the cellar and eat [sic] ravenously, taking his food into his hands." He showed them a ring of Harriet's, a ring William had given her several years before.

"Don't you want it back?" Rulloff said, inscrutably.

"No, give it back to your wife," William told him.

When Rulloff left Lansing, he told his neighbors he was off for an extended trip with his family "between the lakes" and not to look for him for several weeks. At first, people believed his stories. They assumed he had gone to join his wife and child. But after a few weeks, they got suspicious. The departure had been so sudden, and no one had seen Harriet leave, nor had she said anything about an upcoming vacation or an uncle in Motts Corner.

A small group of townspeople entered the Rulloff home to investigate. Very little was gone. The family didn't seem to have packed for an extended trip, and Harriet's clothes from the last day she had been seen were strewn about the living room. The house looked as though it had been escaped, not left for a planned vacation. One detail caught the attention of a town doctor: Harriet's skirt, in a perfect circle on the floor, as if she'd just stepped out of it.

When Rulloff showed up at a store in Ithaca where Ephraim and William were sitting, William asked him if he'd heard that people suspected him of murdering his wife and baby. Rulloff couldn't sleep that night. He told William he was troubled that people thought that about him. Instead of fleeing, though, he went to stay with Harriet's parents. His story had changed. He told her parents that Harriet and the baby had gone ahead to Madison in Lake County, Ohio, where the three of them would make a fresh start.

It appeased Harriet's mother but not her brother Ephraim. He wasn't alone. A group of men came to ask Rulloff some questions. When he refused to answer, they made thinly veiled threats. Ephraim, giving him the benefit of the doubt, suggested that Rulloff write to Harriet and wait for her reply, then they would have proof positive she was alive and well. Rulloff wrote the letter to Harriet in care of "N. Dupuy" in Madison, Ohio. Ephraim showed the letter to the men and went to the post office to mail it. When he returned, Rulloff was gone.

By some accounts Rulloff ran the forty-five miles to Auburn, where there was a railway station, arriving early morning. He arrived at the station a mess, and his state wasn't improved when he came face-to-face with his brother-in-law.

Ephraim, after being duped in Ithaca, had come to arrest him, but Rulloff somehow managed to convince him that he was simply on his way to fetch his wife, having been distressed by her family's worry and the accusations leveled against him. Ephraim went with him.

In Buffalo, Rulloff and Ephraim disembarked the train and headed to the port to catch a steamer to Cleveland. In the crowded confusion of boarding, Rulloff gave his brother-in-law the slip again.

Entertaining the possibility that Rulloff might have gotten lost in the crowd, and not knowing what else to do, Ephraim made his way to Madison, Ohio. No one had heard of Harriet or an "N. Dupuy," and no one knew of a young woman and her infant daughter new in town. Rulloff had merely gone to Cleveland on the next boat. Ephraim rushed back and, improbably, found him in a seedy bar on the docks. This time, Ephraim brought a detective he'd hired and a warrant for his arrest in Cleveland. Instead of sitting in a jail in a strange city, Rulloff agreed to go back to Ithaca with them. On the boat, Harriet's brother leaned on Rulloff to tell him what happened to his sister and niece. Rulloff answered by threatening to throw himself overboard. Ephraim, fed up with the man's games, told him to go right ahead.

Crowds began to gather at the dock. One of the many steamboats that made the trip along Lake Erie between Cleveland and Buffalo would soon arrive. This one, though, was carrying a man they say murdered his wife and baby. News of the apprehension of Edward Rulloff spread quickly; by the time the steamboat Rulloff and Schutt were on pulled into Buffalo, people were there to see them arrive. The two men boarded a train, and when they arrived in Ithaca, more people were waiting. Rulloff wanted to be led to the prison on foot, to see his crowds, but Schutt refused to turn the crime into a spectacle. They made the journey by omnibus, a large horse-drawn carriage with a set fare—the nineteenth-century's commuter transport.

Newspaper illustration of Rulloff

The police searched high and low, and dredged the lakes around Ithaca repeatedly, at a cost of $10,000 (over $320,000 today), but no bodies were found. Rulloff's trial began early in 1846, and he could not be charged with murder. Instead, he was charged with the abduction of his wife. He had defense council but then as later, directed his own strategy and often took the lead in making objections and asking pointless questions of witnesses, possibly to confuse them. His legal tactics stayed consistent throughout his career. He never testified, depending on the lack of evidence to create doubt. In his trial on abduction charges, though, Rulloff was given the harshest sentence possible: ten years of hard labor at Auburn State Prison.

He put the time to good use. In prison, Rulloff returned to his studies, when he wasn't in the workshops, where prisoners performed any number of jobs to offset the cost of their upkeep. He started in the cutlery shop, where he learned to use the emery wheel to sharpen and polish metal—a strange thing to teach a suspected murderer. That workshop closed down, and the prison authorities set him to work designing carpets. Rulloff produced beautiful carpets—and a healthy profit for the prison. It seemed the man really could turn his hand to anything.

Prisoners were allowed to keep small excesses in pay; with his (and additional help from his brother Rulof Rulloffson), Rulloff bought books, even importing some. He discovered his true—one might say, obsessive—passion: philology. The study of the structure and origins of language, philology was esoteric even then and a curious pursuit for a man of his background. He reported that one night in his cell, he

> discovered . . . the secret of success in philological studies, he saw in his mind's eye the outline, the glimpse of his "method in the formation of language" which some bright angel whispered to him was to be . . . the talisman of his fame and future." An epiphany—inspiration or folly—that consumed him till his death.

Despite his mostly good behavior in prison (he was known for passionate outbursts when his crimes were alluded to), and despite the intervening decade, the public still wanted Edward Rulloff's blood. On his release date in 1856, in the office of the warden, the Sheriff of Tompkins County served a second warrant for his arrest on suspicion of murdering his wife. Rulloff simply held out his hands for the handcuffs to be put back on.

○──○──○

The next year and half were consumed with legal wrangling. Rulloff and his counsel claimed a kind of double jeopardy because there was no new evidence. With opinion so deeply against Rulloff, however, he was then charged with his daughter's murder. As Priscilla's body had still not been found, the legal documents covered the bases by charging him with murdering his child by strangulation, bodily assault, and poison.

While the DA was sorting out what to charge him with, Rulloff remained in custody. As decisions and deferrals dragged on, he waited in the Ithaca jail, chained to the floor, kept busy teaching local boys and girls—whose parents had no objection to a free education, even if the teacher was a suspected murderer and the school was the cell block.

Deaf to the warnings of Ephraim Schutt, the warden, Undersheriff Jacob S. Jarvis, sent his son, Albert, to learn at the feet of Rulloff. The whole family lived in the jail building, and Undersheriff Jarvis soon had Rulloff helping him write an autobiography. His prisoner even won the affection of his wife, Jane Jarvis. The warden trusted Rulloff and believed language lessons were paving the way to a bright future for his son. Sixteen-year-old Albert learned more than languages. His relationship with Rulloff set him on the path to ruin.

Rulloff was found guilty of the murder of his daughter. The appeal process lasted a year—a panel of judges on a two-to-one vote let the verdict stand. Rulloff didn't stick around to hear it.

Young Albert Jarvis was indicted for aiding in Rulloff's escape, then released on bail, but there'd been no shortage of other people to help. Two men, Isaac Allen and James Henry, were suspected by the police in the matter. James Henry was briefly jailed but released due to lack of evidence. The sheriff didn't know Rulloff's brother's names: Ruloff Isaac Allen Rulloffson and James Henry Henniger.

At large, Rulloff wandered from place to place. He did millwork for his brother but moved on when things got too hot. A $500 reward was placed on the "learned murderer," then raised to $1,250—over $30,000 today. In the bills posted about him, Rulloff was described as about five foot ten, with a large head, thick neck, several weeks of beard growth, and large hands.

Under the name of James Nelson, he approached Mr. A. B. Richmond, a lawyer and inventor in Meadville, about buying a share in a patent for one of Richmond's machines. Despite the stranger's odd appearance and rough clothing, Richmond was impressed by Rulloff, surprised by his knowledge of conchology (the study of shells), mineralogy, and anatomy. Rulloff spoke to him in perfect Latin, followed by excellent ancient Greek, and pulled from his pocket a certificate claiming he had been examined by the late president of Allegheny College and deemed to be a marvel in languages. He said he hoped to use the certificate to find work as a principal in a school.

In the weeks Rulloff spent with Richmond building a model of the machine, the inventor missed revealing clues. Once, Rulloff described a design for a polishing wheel that Richmond knew to be used at Auburn Prison. Richmond teased, "Mr. Nelson, that is the way they polish cutlery in the penitentiary. Were you ever in there?" Rulloff looked like "a tiger ready to spring upon its victim," before he realized Richmond was joking.

Rulloff was supposedly counting on money from his brother to buy Richmond's patent. When it didn't come through, he asked if the inventor would instead take a number of gold watches. Somehow, Richmond still didn't find anything suspect about his guest. On the contrary, by this time, he was "much attached to the man" and agreed to take those watches in payment.

Rulloff went off on a robbery spree. During one job, he was out in the snow long enough that frostbite set in on his left foot. Despite writing himself a prescription for his frozen foot and filling it in a pharmacy in Jamestown, NY, he lost his big toe.

At a hotel bar in Jamestown, down one toe, Rulloff ran into a fellow convict out of Auburn penitentiary. When they met later in a nearby barn, Rulloff pulled out a three-barreled pistol he himself had invented and threatened the life of his old acquaintance—should he reveal the fugitive's true identity to anyone.

The lure of the $1,250 reward won out. Soon after, Rulloff was captured by the sometimes cross-purpose efforts of the ex-con, a deputy, a farmer, the farmer's wife, a constable, and three neighbors—and some rocks they threw at him. But for the deaths and deceptions, Rulloff's story would read like a farce.

He'd been going by the name Wilcox, teaching writing in a school. Haphazard as this capture was, Rulloff as James Nelson had had his picture taken back in Meadville, and it was used to identify him as a perpetrator of the robberies. Unremarkable now, but at the time, using photography as a clue in solving crime was unusual, if not unheard of. It wouldn't be the last time a photograph would play a role in a case involving Rulloff. But back in custody, a whole different —and revolutionary—technique was about to be used in the quest to convict this murderer once and for all.

○—○—○

Dr. R. Ogden Doremus had just done something cutting edge. As an expert witness in the murder trial of James Stephens in New York in March of 1859, he'd examined and tested the exhumed remains of Stephens' wife for poison. He'd insisted on a special laboratory and dissecting room, new equipment, purified chemicals, and another whole corpse of a woman who'd died in an accident to dissect for comparison. A new technique, it was roundly mocked by the defense. What could be found in the stomach of a body a year dead? Arsenic, it turned out. Stephens was convicted.

Given Rulloff's maddening ability to slip the noose, and the fact that the bodies of Harriet and Priscilla had still not been found, the officials in Ithaca weren't convinced even a conviction of infanticide would bring Rulloff to the gallows. They were looking for a guarantee that he would hang. They exhumed the bodies of two other people Rulloff was suspected of killing, and the prosecution paid a call on Dr. Doremus.

Doremus found copper deposits in the tissues of Amelia Schutt's stomach, but not arsenic. Copper poisoning could certainly cause death, but at that time, doctors routinely used it to treat any number of ailments. Rulloff may have treated Amelia and Amille with copper, but if he did, he'd have been doing what any other doctor might in the situation. If he were using copper as a murder weapon, it was a canny choice. The case was dismissed, and the prosecution fell back onto the conviction in the death of his infant daughter, Priscilla. He was sentenced to hang, but the authorities were right to doubt that his date with the hangman would happen.

Rulloff's new attorney, Finch, convinced the judge more than circumstantial evidence was needed to hang a person. But this simply opened up a new trial. With no new evidence to promise execution, a lynch mob began to form outside the prison. The mob planned to grab Rulloff on his release and hang him. Catching wind of the plot, the sheriff spirited Rulloff out of Ithaca to Auburn for his own safety. The people who'd gathered around the jail to see mob justice served "almost howled in the rage of disappointment."

Rulloff and his lawyer, Finch, held to their one core principle of defense: to hang Rulloff, the proof had to be so irrefutable that no "rational possibility" of another explanation existed. It worked. Frustrating the prosecution and infuriating the public, Rulloff walked free and into a whole new chapter in his criminal life.

7

If Rulloff had ever considered an honest career in law or medicine, those days were over. But he desperately wanted to be a scholar—a profession he couldn't seem to pursue without deceit and criminality.

Once again free and in Pittsburgh, he claimed to be an Oxford academic to secure a teaching job at Jefferson College, only to leave when he heard about better teaching jobs elsewhere. He broke into a jewelry store to pay for the trip. After unknowingly hitching a ride with a horse thief, they were caught, and he claimed the thief had planted the jewels on him. Again, Rulloff walked away. He would later claim, "But for the d—d horse thief I might have been a Professor or President of a Southern College. I am the victim, and always have been, of circumstances." He was a master of self-delusion and of shifting blame onto others for his own transgressions. He seemed to care for no one.

Except Al Jarvis. The bond between the two was strong enough that whenever Al called for help, Rulloff came running. Twice Jarvis wrote him for financial help, and Rulloff dropped everything to assist the young man who'd been his prison student. And when Jarvis again twice called on him, these times from prison, begging for aid, Rulloff got him out —once with bribery, once by acting the lawyer. Before his death, Rulloff explained his earlier dedication to Jarvis by romanticizing the breakout Jarvis had helped bring about. That night long ago, he said he'd made Jarvis a pledge: "If he should ever find himself in need of assistance or a friend, to come to me."

Reunited in New York City, the two men embarked on a life of petty crime. They were moderately successful until a burglary charge landed Rulloff in Sing Sing for two years under the assumed name of James H. Kerron. Known in prison as "Big Jim," Rulloff was mocked for giving his age, upon arrest, as twenty-one—when it was clear he was in his forties. As usual, his varied mechanical and scholarly skills made him useful to prison officials. They made him book-keeper of the cabinet shop; his copperplate penmanship was marvelous and distinct—and would later be used against him.

In Sing Sing he met fellow burglar William T. Dexter, known as Billy. Billy Dexter was poor and illiterate, and easily taken in by Big Jim's magnetism and intelligence. On their release, they formed a criminal band about which one journalist sensationally wrote: "In all criminal annals there is no more romantic and singular trinity than that first completed in Sing Sing prison." The trio worked together for years, on and off, separated now and then by one or the other of them landing in jail. The three men seemed close; there's no evidence there was ever a betrayal between them. They apparently never gave one another up, even to avoid jail time.

They were always incarcerated under false names, gave false ages, and were almost unknown to police, perhaps because of their relative prudence in disposing of their stolen goods. They didn't go to the usual criminal receivers or hang out in the usual criminal haunts.

Jarvis and Dexter saw Rulloff as a kind of master, awed by his learning and intelligence. For the most part, they lived leanly, Rulloff promising the younger men that his scholarship assured them all an imminent bright future. Sometimes the crimes were as mean as stealing potatoes from a field.

After their time in Sing Sing together, Rulloff was living with Dexter at his mother's house on Graham Street in Brooklyn. He arrived, as usual, with a scheme—this time a new way to color photographs. His brother William was a famous and respected photographer out in California; his own experiments in the field fizzled. Billy's sister threw Rulloff's paints into the yard; the neighbor's chickens ate them and died. Rulloff collected rents for the Dexter family and, always eager to inflate his status, boasted about "his" properties in Brooklyn.

Meanwhile, the Civil War raged. All three men were of fighting age, though Rulloff's missing toe might have been a liability. None of them fought. Billy Dexter and his brother, though, embarked on a common Civil War scheme: they would join the army for the commission, then desert before combat, and rejoin elsewhere. Rulloff and Jarvis continued to commit minor burglaries, and when the war was over, in spring 1865, Dexter once again joined his companions in his own house and in their criminal enterprises.

Then, in February 1866, there was a robbery at a silk factory on 35th Street in Manhattan. Silk was a growing industry in the US, even through the war years of increased tariffs. Raw silk fed the hunger for luxuries. New factories were churning out silk thread in precious bundles that were easily transported and made a tidy sum for dry goods merchants. Or thieves. The burglary that had landed Rulloff in Sing Sing was a silk theft. And now the factory on 35th Street had been broken into in the middle of the night, and $2,000 of fabrics stolen, in what would come to seem like a template for Rulloff's final crime.

The watchman on duty was beaten brutally by the burglars and later died. Despite a full investigation, the perpetrators were never found, though officers of the Twentieth Precinct concluded that the robbers were neither professionals nor usually active in the area. Reports said there were three burglars, and two were young, one of them quite good looking. They sounded a lot like Rulloff, Dexter, and Jarvis.

It was all for a noble cause, Rulloff would claim. The aliases, the thefts, the capers, and killings: crime in service of scholarship. When he wasn't off on a heist or fencing the goods, he was working feverishly on a book that would gain him nationwide notoriety. It was inconceivable to him that the book might not be the gold mine and seismic intellectual legacy he was counting on. He built castles on the shifting sands of his intellectual life, but day to day, he depended on more hard-scrabble skills. He was, as journalist Ed Crapsey dubbed him, "The Man of Two Lives."

By the middle of 1866, Rulloff and Jarvis were living largely in two rooms at 19 Delancey Street. Rulloff went by the name E. C. Howard, and his young companion was known as Charles Thompson. Rulloff, apparently, was still teaching Jarvis languages, but sometimes, the two would disappear for days at a time. Poor when they left, on their return, they seemed flush. Otherwise, they were quiet, sober, inoffensive tenants. After a few months, a one-eyed man and two women moved into the rooms with them: "James Henry" (Rulloff's half-brother, James Henniger), the constant confederate of the Rulloffson brothers; Jane Jarvis; and her daughter, Helen. Jane had left her husband, the sheriff, after the escape debacle sent him running to California, and Rulloff's intimacy with the Jarvis family never wavered.

Rulloff's was a peripatetic life during this period. In

various schemes, in various places in New York state, he posed as a priest, a state canvasser, a paralyzed German beggar with the shakes, and his usual credentialed scholar. He acted as a sort of counselor to a gang of bank robbers and enjoyed the fleeting moments in his charades when good society embraced him. He claimed to be "sick of the business."

Rulloff's family in Pennsylvania begged him not to take any more risks but to come live in the country away from the temptations of the city. But he wanted to be near the public libraries in New York: the Astor library, the Eclectic library, and the Mercantile libraries. He said, "I would be perfectly content and happy to be shut up the rest of my life in one of these great libraries." It wasn't the library he was shut up in for much of his adult life, though. Crime—risky and exciting —had become a habit. Laboring in the trees as his brothers Rulof and James did was no draw.

Dexter and Jarvis, too, were traveling around, thieving. In the spring of 1869, they had successfully hit a dry goods mercantile in Binghamton, NY, and come away with a valuable load of silks, which they managed to fence with the help of their one-time housekeeper, Maggie Graham. That summer, Dexter, under the name of Davenport, was caught in another crime. Rulloff went to Cortland, NY, and posing as James Dalton, a lawyer from the city, attempted to spring him from prison by bribing the sheriff. His exploits in Cortland would be used against him later. For Jarvis, the temptation of that mercantile in Binghamton persisted.

By then, Rulloff was deep into his magnum opus, *Method in the Formulation of Language*, the breakthrough in philology he'd conceived lying in his cell back in the Auburn penitentiary. He and Jarvis had moved to 170 3rd Avenue, their final home in New York. Rulloff now went as Edouard Leurio and Jarvis as Charles G. Curtis. Rulloff presented himself as the renowned philologist he believed he would soon be and Jarvis as a "Commercial Traveller." Rulloff and Jarvis had nothing, at this point, but books. Some of them were rare, but Rulloff never sold them even in extremis.

The house on Third Avenue was owned by the Jacobs family, who took a liking to their studious tenant. Mrs. Jacobs told her son he should try to be more like Mr. Leurio, who they called the "Professor," and she allowed her daughter to sit with the man almost daily. Leurio and Thompson were, once again, almost perfect lodgers, with little drinking, no late nights, and no company.

Late into the night or wee hours almost daily, a light could be seen shining from his room, as he sat at his desk and scratched away at his masterpiece. Jarvis and Dexter supported his work by robbing all over the area, stashing the goods for Rulloff to fence. He promised them riches once he sold his book.

In June 1869, the "Professor" issued a circular that appeared in the New York papers. It offered for sale a manuscript "of peculiar interest, disclosing a beautiful and unsuspected method in language spoken and read by millions of our race." The asking price? $500,000—over $7,000,000 today, an absurd amount of money. An editorial in the *Nation* later observed, "A very wild lunatic, indeed, it would be who should hope to get five hundred thousand dollars from any assembly of philologists of the United States."

Rulloff, as Leurio, showed up in July at a convention of the American Philological Society in Poughkeepsie and insisted a committee be appointed to consider his manuscript. He'd already thoroughly exasperated the philologists in the city, some of whom were at the meeting, but they agreed to consider his theory. The reason they gave for ultimately rejecting his manuscript was that it did not fall "within the bounds of the convention"—a euphemism if ever there was one. Rulloff, true to form, felt misunderstood—a victim—though he had been given a hearing. In a letter to the editor of the *New York Times,* eminent philologist G. F. Comfort assailed Rulloff and his theory, saying he "did violence to all historical truth." Comfort described his behavior at the meeting: "the mild and gentle Mr. Leurio disappeared. In his place appeared the violent, abusive, and profane Mr. Leurio." Jekyll and Hyde.

Rulloff had convinced Jarvis and Dexter—and was himself convinced—that the Convention was going to laud his paper (the basis of his greater work) as revolutionary, and that fame and fortune would follow. Billy Dexter, not fully understanding the situation, but feeling keenly the disappointment on his friend's and his own behalf, told his brother John that Rulloff (he called him Jim from their Sing Sing days) had "taken his book before Congress, but the congressmen hadn't sense enough to see that it was worth publishing." He said that Jim was going to publish it himself and he, Billy, would get the money to do it. There was only one way Billy Dexter supported the studies of his compatriot. Never had a philological theory led to so much larceny.

On the heels of this disappointment, Rulloff received a letter in August from Jarvis, who was once again in Binghamton casing the store where he'd found such success that spring. He wrote that a new shipment of silk had arrived. He had the Halbert Brothers store once more in his crosshairs.

The circus had come to town. Tents were going up, and strange people wandered the streets of Binghamton. The late afternoon buzzed with summer and anticipation, when the train on the Erie Railway line arrived from New York City. Rulloff, Dexter, and Jarvis stepped onto the platform and into the surprise of the circus. They should have found out about it ahead of time, an uneasy Rulloff told Billy Dexter.

They slept in the barn of the county poor house, and the next day in town, the superintendent of the poor house recognized Rulloff from his days working as a pharmacy clerk in Ithaca. It was too dangerous, Rulloff kept telling his partners the day they struck. He wanted to back out—go back to the city. Jarvis, his mind fixed on this heist, berated him. Rulloff never could say no to Al Jarvis. He stayed.

They knew that the store on the river's edge was being renovated and was poorly secured. They also knew of the two night guards in the store, but they intended to sneak past them as they slept, dosing them with chloroform, and leave them none the wiser until morning.

Between midnight and one a.m. the men entered the store. Once inside, Dexter and Rulloff removed their shoes for stealth (Jarvis had worn rubber boots) and pulled masks over their faces. They made it upstairs to the silks, and began piling the most valuable outside. Merrick rolled over in bed, and Rulloff commented to Dexter that Jarvis hadn't used enough chloroform.

Just then, downstairs, Jarvis tripped over something and made a racket. The guards woke up; Merrick grabbed his gun. He pointed it at Rulloff's chest and pulled the trigger—click, click, click—three times. The gun wouldn't go off. He rushed Rulloff "like a demon." Jarvis and Rulloff made it back downstairs, but Dexter had been caught. Merrick and Burrows had him down on the ground, beating him. Jarvis fired up the stairs, nicking some wood that flew into Burrow's face. The guard fell back, thinking he'd been shot. Merrick grabbed Jarvis and bent him backward over a counter, grabbing him by the genitals. Jarvis screamed to Rulloff, "for God's sake, take him off; he is killing me." Rulloff shot Merrick in the head.

They hadn't expected the guards to fight so hard.

While the alarm was being raised, and the town of Binghamton was being woken from its slumber, the trio were escaping through the back of the department store. In their haste to get out, they left several items behind, including a very strange left shoe.

KILLER GENIUS

Newspaper illustration of the crime

○─○─○

The men ran for the river, hoping to cross with ease, as it was the height of summer. But both Dexter and Jarvis were injured. Dexter was bleeding so badly from a head wound, he couldn't see. He also couldn't swim. Neither, apparently, could Jarvis.

Once found, and dragged out of the water and into the August heat, their bodies started to bloat and darken. Before taking them to be embalmed, Seneca Bullock, a local photographer, was called in to take their picture. Crime scenes not being the secured areas they are today, the townspeople gathered to examine the bodies, propped up on planks against a barn to get the best light. No one knew them. Everyone knew by this time, however, that there had been three burglars. The race was on to find the third man.

Police went through all of the town's usual suspects: known thieves and brawlers and those down on their luck. The Chenango River and its banks were searched thoroughly, investigators figuring that if two of their suspects had drowned, then the third might have also.

Blockades were set up on the roads out of the city. At the Erie Railway Bridge, a man approached and was stopped by officers. Upon questioning, he claimed to be on his way to New York City but said that he had been ejected from his train at Binghamton for lack of funds—and now was attempting to walk there. Those manning the picket told the walker that he would be detained for questioning, which he agreed to—until, that is, a freight train crossed the bridge. The man made a dash for it, at risk to life and limb, and cleared the train, disappearing into the midnight gloom.

A search for the mystery man went on until morning. There were fears he had somehow jumped aboard the train, though this would have taken impossible strength and speed. Eventually, he was found hiding in an outhouse. He had smeared himself with mud and dirt, but despite this, it was clear his shirtfront was stained with blood. He was taken back to the cells of the police station. When the man was examined, no weapons were found upon his person, just a key and, in one of his pockets, a ticket—not to the city but heading away from it. The ticket to Batavia was unused, as though this strange, mud-streaked man had been planning to get away.

10

Judge Ransom Balcom was as curious as anybody else in Binghamton about the stunning murder at Halberts. He was among the crowd when Rulloff was brought before the coroner's jury taking evidence in the case. He wanted to see what manner of rogue had committed such a crime. Judge Balcom had been the lone dissenting voice on the panel of three judges who had voted to let the guilty verdict in the murder of Rulloff's daughter stand. Balcom had come to his opinion back then based on the lack of evidence in the case, an adherence to the rule of law—not necessarily because he believed Rulloff was innocent.

In the Binghamton court room, he recognized the suspect immediately. "You are Edward H. Rulloff; you murdered your wife and child in Lansing in 1845," he said.

Rulloff had been staunchly maintaining his story that he was just an innocent trying to make his way on foot to New York. He'd coolly looked at the laid-out corpses of the burglars, even asked to walk around them for the best view, and claimed he'd never seen them before. He refused to engage on the ticket from New York to Batavia that was in his possession. When he was first detained, he'd given his name as "Charles Augustus." To the coroner's jury he claimed his name was George Williams—until Judge Balcom spoke up.

37

It didn't faze Rulloff at all. "There, gentlemen," he said,

> you have an explanation of my strange conduct. Knowing of my misfortunes in this portion of New York, you can understand why I was anxious, being here accidentally when a murder was committed, to pass through the city without my identity being known. You know the proverb, gentlemen, about the results of giving a dog a bad name.

With his usual *sangfroid,* he was using the proverb "give a dog an ill name, and he is half hanged" to justify his slipperiness. Upon identifying Rulloff, Judge Balcom had turned to the coroner's jury and warned, "This man understands his rights better than you do and will defend them to the last." The coroner, the DA, and the jury found Rulloff's explanation plausible anyway. They let him go.

○−○−○

Moving fast, Rulloff made it five miles out of town in the hour since he'd left the courtroom before they caught up with him again. Someone, just after Rulloff's departure, had remembered something about his left big toe. He didn't have one.

At the crime scene, the perpetrators had left a pair of shoes of a type called Oxford ties. The left shoe had an indentation in the area of the left big toe. Additionally, rags had been stuffed into the missing toe's place. Once they'd put these two things together, the police went after him.

The sheriff made Rulloff remove his left boot (he was wearing Jarvis's rubber boots) to reveal the missing toe and took him back to town. In a macabre twist on the Cinderella story, they made him try on the shoe; it was a perfect fit. It was enough to take him into custody but not enough to convict him of the murder—thus began an exhaustive and systematic investigation to gather evidence linking Rulloff to the dead burglars. First, the police discovered that one of the dead men pulled from the river had on his person a ticket from New York to Batavia, for the same date as the ticket Rulloff was carrying.

Next, they discovered that Rulloff had been rooming with one of the dead men, Jarvis, and had been imprisoned with Dexter, the other. The jaws of the law were closing in around him.

Edward Rulloff's timber baron brother, Ruloff, hired the esteemed attorney George Becker to defend him. With his signature self-confidence, Rulloff offered to write an autobiography to fund his own defense. His brother insisted on just paying.

Among the detectives working the case, the general consensus was that they had gotten their man. The main investigating officers, Captain Hedden and Detective Reilley, worked tirelessly to give the prosecution an airtight case—something they all knew they needed, given Rulloff's almost uncanny ability to slip out of the grip of the law.

Ultimately, they found unequivocal links between the three men. Rulloff collected rent for Jarvis's mother; he'd been instrumental in getting huge amounts of silk, that Dexter had stolen, dyed. Dexter had also had a scrap of paper in his pocket upon which the name of an attorney was scrawled. When detectives followed this name to New York City, they showed the man, attorney William Thornton, the picture of the corpses. He ID'd Billy Dexter and directed them to an address in Brooklyn, where they found a tumbledown house. The resident was an elderly woman, seeming a little confused by the intrusion; she said she hadn't seen Mr.

Dexter in months and that an agent had been sent to collect rent instead. Officers showed her a picture of Rulloff. Why yes, the old woman said, "that's the agent!"

A strong connection between the men was impossible to deny.

11

Jail apparently agreed with Rulloff by now. Four months had passed between his final capture and the official beginning of his trial. It was said that when they incarcerated him, he looked sixty, but at the start of his trial, he looked forty-five. He was actually fifty-two. He'd been living rough. Rougher, it seemed, than prison.

Reporter Ed Crapsey—who went on to write the lurid and damning account of Rulloff's life and trial, *The Man of Two Lives*—would claim that after Rulloff's final arrest, his dead wife's mother, Hannah Schutt, was brought to the prison to identify him. Twenty-five years before, Rulloff had predicted that Mrs. Schutt would go down "in sorrow to the grave." At the jail, in Rulloff's presence, as Crapsey told it, she was "so overcome by the sight of the destroyer that her frail hold on life was loosened and she died a few days afterward." True or not, it seemed to confirm for some the scale and fascination of Rulloff's evil.

His infamy grew. The case was huge. It was covered in full by *The New York Times* and, more influential at the time, the *New-York Tribune*. The Binghamton *Democratic Leader* scooped everybody by being first on the scene when the bodies were pulled out of the water. Ham Freeman, the *Leader*'s reporter, would go on to publish an account—often sympathetic, or at least more nuanced than other profiles—of Rulloff's life, as well as a lengthy interview with and confession by Rulloff himself.

Crowds gathered daily outside the prison to try to catch a glimpse of the genius killer. He had a famously large head, which phrenologists pounced on as a sign of his genius. Some even argued a genius couldn't be a killer, as the theories of criminality of the time held that criminals were akin to primitive beasts. Rulloff presented a conundrum. By some reckonings, if he was a killer, he was faking being a genius. If he were an actual genius, he couldn't be a killer. Meanwhile, the case was brought to trial.

Mirroring the trio of criminals, the prosecution was a mighty triumvirate led by attorney Peter Hopkins, of whom the NYPD's Captain Hedden said, "Hopkins is worth more as a detective than all the detectives in my precinct." Joining him were Attorney General Marshall B. Champlain, a canny player in state politics, and Lewis Seymour, a former congressman and influential Binghamton lawyer. By contrast, the defense seemed wan. Binghamton attorney George Becker, relatively young and used to defending seeming lost causes, brought on Charles L. Beale, a former congressman. But Beale was unwell and brought little in the way of effective counsel to the defense table.

The circumstances of the crime put to the jury were that Dexter, Jarvis, and Rulloff had broken into Halberts around midnight, and after a physical altercation, one of them—though it was unclear who—had shot Merrick. Merrick had been killed—his colleague, wounded. The three robbers fled to attempt a river crossing. Jarvis and Dexter drowned, possibly due to their injuries. In his opening statement, prosecutor Hopkins, also told the jury the story of Rulloff's checkered past, including the deaths of Harriet and Priscilla Rulloff. Although Becker objected (on Rulloff's insistence) that the defendant's past was beyond the scope of the trial, the jury had heard the details.

The prosecutor offered two pieces of evidence placing Rulloff at and near the scene of the crime. The shoe—the Oxford tie—with a dent in the toe, which fit Rulloff's deformed foot perfectly. Second, a *New York Times* with an article cut out of it had been found in a satchel discarded in a swamp a mile out of town. A clipping of that article—on the Prussia policy—was found in Rulloff's rooms. The shoe, Rulloff knew they had; the clipping came as a surprise. He "started in his seat, and a spasm of dread passed over his face."

To finish his remarks, Hopkins spoke of Frederick Merrick, dying a hero's death, of once innocent Al Jarvis, led into temptation and a "felon's death," and of Merrick's mother, already widowed, now with another sorrow to carry. Once he'd brought to the jury's attention the earlier miscarriage of justice that had allowed a murderer to escape the gallows, but which would not happen again here, he sat.

Newspaper illustration of Frederick Merrick

The prosecution started their questioning with Gilbert Burrows, the surviving night guard. Burrows told the court about the building work going on at the time of the break in, allowing the robbers to easily and quietly bore through a single-layer door set in wood and plaster. Burrows went on to detail the masks, ropes, and other items left by the robbers in the store, as well as the infamous shoe, when something unexpected happened. Rulloff stood and, bypassing his attorney entirely, objected on a legal point.

The items found in the store, he said, could not be used in evidence until it had been unequivocally proven that he had been one of the three men there. It was a perfectly valid attempt, and genuine case law backed it up, but Lewis Seymour, of the prosecution's team, countered that the links between the evidence would become clear in the course of the prosecution's case.

Judge Hogeboom let the examination of the witness proceed. George Becker unexpectedly announced that the defendant himself was to question the young guard. Rulloff, again playing the lawyer, directed his cross-examination to the notion of self-defense in the hope of a lesser sentence. He and his attorneys alleged that the clerk had responded with disproportionate violence to a non-violent crime. He'd later describe Mirrick as acting like a "perfect demon." In essence, Rulloff was claiming to have been the victim of an assault to which the shooting had been a natural response—if he'd done it. Which he hadn't. Jarvis, he claimed, was the shooter. At the time, though, Jarvis was bent backwards over the counter, screaming, with his genitals in Merrick's grip. More muddled still, the defense's strategy seemed also to rest on the claim that Rulloff hadn't even been in Binghamton at the time of the robbery.

Burrows insisted he'd gotten a good look: Rulloff was the man who'd shot Merrick. Rulloff questioned Burrows about his testimony that he had seen Rulloff "square in the face" after he'd shot Merrick. He asked the clerk whether the light was good in the store.

Burrows answered, with more innocence than snark, "You know what the light was." The gallery clapped and cheered.

In its quest to positively identify the dead men, the prosecution used the photograph Seneca Bullock had taken of Jarvis and Dexter the day they'd been pulled out of the water. Photography was still in its infancy as a crime-solving tool, and the defense tried to throw doubt on the reliability of the photograph. In a cross-examination of Bullock, George Becker asked him if the bodies looked natural and whether "they had the appearance of dead persons?" Bullock answered, "They resembled dead persons very closely, I should judge." The prosecution used the photograph over and over in their examination of witnesses, asking them to identify one or the other of the bodies in the picture.

Across the country, Rulloff's younger brother, famed San Francisco photographer, William Herman Rulloffson, had anticipated that photography would someday aid in criminal justice. He couldn't know how close to home his prediction would hit.

12

Strange things emerged from the pockets of dead Billy Dexter. Aside from the piece of paper with attorney William Thornton's name on it, the police had found a note that appeared to be a key to a mysterious shorthand, a system that Rochester shorthand reporter William H. Osgoodby testified was unlike any he had ever encountered—though he knew over two hundred systems. Writings taken from Rulloff's room, including the lecture on phrenology he'd given back in Lansing over two decades before, were written in the same shorthand, apparently devised by Rulloff, and matched the handwriting in the note in Dexter's pocket. The system, Osgoodby claimed, could not be read without that key.

The other thing found on Billy Dexter was a book called *The Oraculum, or Napoleon Buonaparte's Book of Fate*, a system of divination supposedly used by Napoleon to make decisions and found in the general's "Cabinet of Curiosities at Leipsic [sic]." The prosecution called the twelve-year-old son of the former sheriff of Cortland County to testify about the book. The boy's father, the sheriff, had already testified that Rulloff, posing as attorney James Dalton, had tried to bribe him to release Dexter (at the time using the name William Davenport) from the prison in Cortland. Now the sheriff's son would testify to the fact that he and Dexter (like Rulloff and Jarvis) had developed a friendly relationship, and the boy had sent all the way to New York City for the *Oraculum* he'd given the prisoner. The book found on Dexter, the boy said, looked to be the one he'd given him. The introduction (actually titled, "Advertisement") to the slim book, after establishing that Napoleon had used it on every important occasion, goes on to warn in italics, *"happy had it been for him, had he abided or been ruled by the answers of this Oracle."* Either Napoleon hadn't consulted the Oracle before Waterloo or it hadn't worked. Apparently, the same held true for Billy Dexter.

The prosecution was doing everything in its power to connect Rulloff to the other robbers. They piled on witnesses to prove that the three were close companions in the city and confederates in crime. Moreover, Rulloff's impostures were coming back to haunt him in the form of characters from his past testifying to knowing him by assumed names. A judge who'd once defended him took the stand to compare several signatures on legal documents, all recording different names, and declared them to have been written by Rulloff. Such handwriting analysis is still used in court today, but under the stringent protocols of forensic science, employing highly trained analysts in a laboratory setting. It's unlikely that in the nineteenth century the same care would have been put into matching handwriting samples. Still, it represented an important piece of evidence in Rulloff's case.

Police officers testified to the evidence found in the discarded satchel and in Rulloff's rooms, including burglar's tools, the *New York Times* and the missing article, the samples of shorthand, and a large manuscript—Rulloff's philological masterpiece. When given into his hands in the courtroom, Rulloff "seemed almost to fondle it," and told the judge, "There is the Proof, your Honor, that my occupation does not send me around the country breaking open stores. There is a book that five hundred men in ten years cannot produce."

Throngs of people, spurred by the wide newspaper coverage, were daily queueing and jostling for a place in the gallery. The crowd was not composed of the "roughs" usually found at the courthouse. The men in the audience were well dressed and middle class; a large cohort of women, described as "[ladies] in the true meaning of that much abused word" watched the proceedings with rapt interest, despite the long hours.

Rulloff didn't disappoint. He would object before his lawyer had a chance, and he couldn't resist a bit of drama. When the former sheriff of Cortland County told the court about the bribery episode, Rulloff jumped up to object that such an incident could have no bearing on the present case. Prosecutor Hopkins countered that he was trying to establish that there was more than an attorney-client relationship between Rulloff and Dexter, given that he'd used his own money for a bribe. Rulloff bristled and retorted that he would do as much for a client as Hopkins, if he had the resources of the state behind him. "Damn such evidence," he muttered.

The court heard medical testimony about Rulloff's odd foot, as well as the perfection of the feet of the drowned men —who would not have worn the dented shoe—the effect of the bullet on Merrick's head, and the cause of death. On cross examination, the defense, suggesting that Merrick might have died of shock if he had heart disease, got the doctors who'd examined his body to admit that they had seen cases in which people with bullet wounds to the head survived. On redirect, the prosecution disposed of that tact handily with the testimony of one of the doctors, who said that while Merritt didn't show any symptoms of heart disease, he showed "all the signs of a person dying from compression of the brain, caused by a pistol shot wound."

George Becker must have been pulling his hair out, as, bit by bit; the evidence the prosecution presented undermined his defense strategy before he'd even had a chance to present the case. Becker took an unusual—and perhaps desperate—step for the time: he charged that Rulloff had been abused by the prosecution and the police when they attempted to take a mug shot. Rulloff kept distorting his face in an effort to resist being identified in a photograph, despite the fact that he'd already posed for a photograph as James Nelson back in Meadville. The police applied pliers to his ears and eventually chloroformed him and took the picture while he was unconscious.

The tact didn't have the desired effect; it just made the defendant look guiltier. And, to what must have been Becker's infinite despair, when Rulloff cross-examined the prosecution's last witness, he couldn't help himself—he had to show off. Detective Philip Reilly had just definitively linked Rulloff to Dexter with a letter found in a drawer in Dexter's room. It was in Rulloff's hand addressed to the dead burglar. Rulloff took the opportunity to lecture the courtroom on improved drill bits of his invention, such as the one found in the back door of Halberts. This gave the prosecution the opportunity on redirect to show that several of the same bits had been found in Dexter's drawer with the letter.

From this anemic vantage, the defense would begin presenting its case.

13

Finally, George Becker would get a chance to do his own job. It was half past three on the fourth day of the trial when the defense officially began. In his opening speech, Becker spoke to both the great intelligence and learning of his client—and his misfortunes and poverty. The case against him was unfairly stacked, Becker argued, because of the brimming coffers of the county and the district attorney's corresponding ability to bring in almost everyone who had ever had contact with Rulloff. Rulloff, on the other hand, was a man of vast intellectual, but minimal financial, means. He claimed, too, a popular prejudice the likes of which no prisoner had ever before encountered. His client was a "mild, inoffensive old man of studious and reflective habits."

The twin pillars of Becker's defense strategy were that Rulloff was not in Binghamton on the night of the murder and that whoever did kill Merrick, had done so in unpremeditated self-defense. If he couldn't prove that Rulloff had been elsewhere, he would rely on the unnecessary force argument.

Becker claimed that a witness whose testimony had led to Rulloff's arrest had been wholly incorrect in his belief that Rulloff had entered his store on the day of the robbery, asking for the best whiskey, regardless of price. While Rulloff was in custody, the man mistaken for the defendant had shown up in the store again, telling the owner he was a drover from the West. Further, Becker claimed that Rulloff had been to Buffalo and Batavia after New York City and had not even been in Binghamton on August 16, the night in question.

Following this opening argument, witnesses were called. Very few of them showed up. Becker asked the judge that the testimonies of two doctors who'd taken the stand for the prosecution be stricken from the record because they did not answer the defense's call to the stand. "What do you wish to prove by these witnesses?" said Judge Hogeboom.

"That the hair of this murdered man was not scorched or burnt, and that the pistol could not have been held close to his head." The judge refused to strike the doctors' previous testimonies and said that another witness had already testified to the fact that he'd seen no scorch marks or burns on Merrick's hair. Becker, though, was making a point important to Rulloff's defense. If the shooter had come right up behind Merrick and shot him at close range, there would be scorch marks from the gun and, potentially, evidence of premeditation. If, however, there were no scorch marks, no proof Merrick had been shot at close range, it might support a distant, and perhaps unpremeditated, shot. If the judge would not strike the doctors' testimonies, would the prosecution concede on the record the fact of there being no scorch marks? Before the prosecution could answer, the judge called it unnecessary.

Becker turned to questioning witnesses about Burrows and his confusion following his ordeal. One witness, Francis Farnham, testified he and Burrows had a conversation in the store in which Burrows told him there were two burglars and he couldn't identify either of them. On cross-examination, though, Hopkins brought out the fact that Burrows hadn't been in the store when Farnham claimed to have spoken to him. Another witness, Lyman Clark, sitting in front of the American Hotel on the night of the crime, heard shots and then saw Burrows run out of the front door of Halberts shouting, "Murder!" When Clark and police Chief Flinn came to assist, Burrows said they would have to go round back because the front was locked. Clark told Burrows he knew the front door was open because he'd just seen him come out of it. Only after they pushed open the door and went in, did Burrows say he remembered coming out the front.

The crowd on the sixth day of court, the day when closing arguments would begin, was larger than ever, and at moments when Rulloff seemed particularly uncomfortable, there were rounds of applause. In a pause in proceedings caused by the absence of defense witnesses, Rulloff rose and again began harping on the idea that he could not be tied to the robbers in the water and therefore could not be tied to the robbery and murder. Judge Hogeboom interrupted him to point out that Burrows's testimony proved his presence. Despite admonishing the courtroom during eruptions that his was not a court of public opinion, it wouldn't be the last time this judge's bias would play a role in Rulloff's trial.

Discrediting inconsistencies in Burrows's testimony was uphill work. The direction and depth of bullet holes called into question some details of Burrows's account, and by now, it seemed that trauma may have clouded or adjusted his memories, but the extent of this was not clear. The prosecution had already done a good job answering discrepancies that came up, and after all the evidence they'd presented against Rulloff, leaning on Burrow's confusion to save his client from the gallows was a shaky ladder for Becker to stand on.

Finally, in a strange move on Becker's part, Dr. Daniel Burr, the doctor who had embalmed Dexter and Jarvis, was called to perform an examination of Rulloff's foot in full view of the jury. The aim was to prove that Rulloff's foot was not in fact deformed. His foot was perfectly shaped, it was true, but he was also definitely missing his big toe. In his questioning of Dr. Burr, Rulloff once again showed off his erudition by using words like "phalanx" and "protuberance" instead of "toe." The defense could argue that this was not a deformity and the foot didn't necessarily fit the shoe until they were blue in the face, but it was clear to the jury it did.

Beales, Rulloff's second lawyer, did very little to help his client's case in his closing statement. He maligned the difficulties of being up against huge public prejudice. He then all but admitted that a connection between Rulloff and the drowned burglars had been established. The brunt of Beales's argument dealt once again with the inconsistencies in Burrows's testimony and ability to recall the events of the robbery. He claimed Burrows had been in a "frenzy."

Beales tried to repair the jury's view of his client's character. Rulloff had led, according to the defense's narrative, a quiet domestic life for several years in the bosom of the Jacobses' home. He talked of his prodigious intellectual talents and the fact that he was almost entirely self-taught. His client was, additionally, unknown to the police of New York. Given all this, how could they suppose Rulloff to lead the double life of a thief and murderer? This argument worked only if the jury didn't believe the evidence of Rulloff's pseudonyms and assumed identities, of course.

The evidence found in Rulloff's desk, such as burgling tools, Beales accused no one in particular of planting to frame his client. And finally, the legal issue of murder versus manslaughter he addressed by drawing the jury's attention to the unwarranted and felonious violence of the attack by the clerks on the three burglars, despite the fact that the judge had already expressed the opinion in court that the clerks had every right to kill the burglaries. What, Judge Hogeboom had asked, were they supposed to do?

Beales spoke for four hours, an impressive rhetorical feat, but the defense knew how fragile their case was, how robust the case of the prosecution, and how unpopular their client. Beales ended his closing argument by asking the jury to show mercy.

14

Despite the bitter cold on that January morning, thousands pressed to get into the courtroom on the seventh, and last, day of the Rulloff trial. It opened with Judge Hogeboom inviting the prosecution to present their closing remarks.

Attorney General Champlain was ambitious, a rising star in the Democratic Party. The theater of his closing for the prosecution may have been as much for the press lining the front benches as for the jury. He assured his audience that, contrary to the defense's claims that he brought the full weight and power of his position to bear against the humble defendant, he was there simply to present the facts. He addressed the complaints of public prejudice with a kind of "love the sinner, hate the sin" argument and plainly laid out once more the evidence as the prosecution had presented it. But he also engaged in one very clever, very effective piece of rhetoric.

His premise was that the murder of Frederick Merrick was premeditated because criminals conspiring to burgle have the intent to sweep away anything or anybody that gets in their way. So first, by this logic, it didn't matter who pulled the trigger to kill Merrick, for conspiracy makes them all equally culpable. Second—and this was subtle—he described Rulloff in the act of shooting Merrick: Rulloff came up behind the clerk and, grabbing his head *and turning it slightly*, shot him.

There is no evidence to show that Rulloff turned the head of Merrick in a gesture of cold-blooded premeditation, but it didn't matter. Champlain, with this one imagined flight of rhetoric, had put in the jury's minds that fateful gesture. If the crime was premeditated, even the merest moment ahead of the shot, first-degree murder would be the punishment. That's what Champlain was counting on.

In a charge to the jury filled with bias, Judge Hogeboom cherry-picked pieces of evidence to bring to their attention, paying special heed to the dented Oxford tie, and though he told them it was Rulloff's right not to testify, he indirectly inserted a question into their minds. If he were innocent, why wouldn't he? He finished with a flourish about truth:

> She may be for a time defeated and overcome; she may be obscured by the clouds of ignorance, of sophistry, and of falsehood, but she will ultimately assert her supremacy and shine forth in the undimmed brightness of her nature . . . bringing light out of darkness, order out of confusion, and sooner or later, assert her irresistible power in all the transactions of men.

After the lengthy charge, it took the jury four and a half hours and six ballots to come to a unanimous verdict. But outside the courthouse, fears that Rulloff would once again slip through the grip of the law gave rise to talk of mob justice. Before the trial even began, Will Schutt warned that a Tompkins County posse, two hundred men strong, was ready to mobilize and see justice done if the jury didn't return a guilty verdict. George Becker knew the rumors—he and his clerks were armed along with the sheriff and deputies, just in case.

The whole courtroom seemed to hold its breath, waiting for the foreman to answer the clerk of the court's question: "Gentlemen of the jury, have you agreed upon your verdict?"

"We have," Hiram Mosher, the foreman, answered. Edward H. Rulloff, the jury declared, was guilty of murder in the first degree. Each juryman was asked; each answered: guilty.

Clapping broke out in the gallery and was swiftly silenced by Judge Hogeboom.

Rulloff's affect during the trial was of keen interest to the press. Ringing as much drama as they could out of the spectacle, papers breathlessly reported on his reaction. Each journalist, though, interpreted his emotions differently. Waiting for the verdict to be announced, the *Ithaca Journal* reported that Rulloff "manifested intense excitement," but when the verdict was announced, "he assumed the appearance of one entirely unconcerned." The *New York Times* saw it differently: "Rulloff . . . sank back in his seat, seemingly for the first time overpowered and exhausted." But when the time came for him to be led back to his cell, most observers agreed he looked straight-backed and confident.

During sentencing, Rulloff seemed nonchalant, flipping through some law books. When asked if he had any reasons that the death sentence should not be leveled against him, Rulloff said, "it is not deemed advisable to say anything at present." As Judge Hogeboom advised him to repent, lest he soon be in the next life, Rulloff stood, smiling, one hand in his pocket. The hanging was set for March 3. He sat and laughed with his defense counsel, as if he'd just been set free.

Edward Hamilton Freeman, "Ham" to his friends, was sworn to silence. He wasn't a big city reporter—the *Binghamton Leader* was no *New-York Herald*—and he was young, but he was the first journalist on the scene of the drowned robbers and, it turned out, would be the last journalist to talk to Rulloff before his death. He'd followed the trial with journalistic doggedness, then increasingly, with personal fascination. "There was . . . a magnetism about the man," he would write. He couldn't decide whether Rulloff was "insane, or else the very incarnation of all that is devilish and wicked" but either way, found that his "deranged intellect" made him "not morally or legally accountable for his deeds." But by the time Rulloff was sentenced, Freeman was an intimate of the murderer's—perhaps the only one, since Jarvis and Dexter were dead.

The verdict, if anything, had served to plunge Rulloff even deeper into his philological obsession. When he wasn't working with his counsel on the appeal strategy, he was working on his manuscript. Some described Rulloff's cell as almost pleasant, with plenty of light and air and furniture, his diet limited only by his whims. Others described a dark, claustrophobic vault where the prisoner worked on his manuscript by the dim light of a kerosene burner.

Rulloff took to going half naked in his cell. When one of his guards asked him about it, Rulloff said, as if it were obvious, that when one is imprisoned (as he had been so often) and therefore deprived of exercise, nakedness helps preserve the health of the body. He took care to point out his well-muscled physique, even at the age of fifty-two, as evidence of this. The guard was only really worried that he had to warn his charge whenever a visitor was arriving to give Rulloff time to dress.

Freeman was a regular visitor to the prison, where he and Rulloff spent long hours talking. Only reporters truly interested in his work got in to see him. Others tried and were rebuffed. A reporter from the *New-York Herald* managed to talk his way in, past an apparently jolly sheriff: "Ha! ha! ha! ho! ho! o! o! o!..! You are from the *Herald* and want to see Rulloff? Ha! ha! Why, the *Times* and the *World* sent men here and Rulloff would not see them!"

That reporter stroked Rulloff's vanity by saying the *Herald* was anxious to see the manuscript published; Rulloff was eager to share his obsession. "A hatched egg can no more refuse to emit a chicken than I can abstain from writing on languages." The minute the reporter asked a poorly disguised question on Rulloff's thoughts about his death, though, the prisoner jumped up, pressed his "infernal" face to the bars, and hissed at the man. "Now I know you. You have deceived me; you don't want to know about my book. You want to question me on matters on which I will not speak. Begone, Sir!"

Freeman befriended Rulloff early in the trial and repeatedly showed good faith, bringing to print a series of articles by Rulloff in the *Leader* explaining his theory of language—one a week, from January 20 to May 19 of 1871, the last appearing after Rulloff was dead. Others may have more widely publicized Rulloff's work (to Freeman the theory was "clear . . . as mud"), but he had gained Rulloff's trust. Enough, at any rate, to get the man to confess to his murders. Rulloff swore Freeman to secrecy, a vow the journalist kept until, close to death, Rulloff released him from it.

Rulloff took Freeman back to 1845, to the night of Harriet's death. They'd argued, he told the journalist, over Rulloff's desire to go west. He had wanted to quit practicing medicine and head to Ohio where he would in time become a professor or a lawyer. Harriet could keep the household in Lansing going until he sent for her.

Harriet told him she would never go that far away from her family. He could go, but she was going back home to them. He accused her of really wanting to go to her cousin, Dr. Bull, with whom he was convinced she was in love. He recalled saying that "she might go to h—l if she chose to, but that she should not take the child . . . ."

He tried to wrest baby Priscilla from her arms, but Harriet wouldn't let her go. In a rage, Rulloff said, he grabbed a pestle he used to crush medicine and dealt his wife a blow to the head. He was young and strong; the pestle broke through her skull into her brain. She fell to the floor with the child crying in her arms. He lifted the baby onto the bed and administered "a narcotic to stop its crying" and then tended to Harriet, doing "everything [he] could to restore her."

Freeman reported Rulloff's agitation during the telling of his story—the "cold drops of perspiration" on his brow—his cries of anguish: "'Oh! That dreadful horror! that horrible moment which I would have given worlds to blot out!'" Rulloff paints for him a dramatic picture of his despair as he tried to save his wife and realized he was a doomed man. He mixed up a dram of poison to kill himself, but as with his suicide threat on the ferry with Ephraim Schutt, he couldn't do it. Instead, he put the body in the trunk, drove it to Lake Cayuga, rowed it out to the center, and dropped it, laden with weights, over the side of the boat.

Rulloff studiously avoided mentioning his daughter in his

confession, and Freeman never pressed him very far on the subject. Rulloff made it clear he wouldn't talk about the child with any specificity. There was another Priscilla in the family (other than Rulloff's mother): his niece, the daughter of his brother Rulof Rulloffson. She was around the same age as the lost infant, and seemed, to Freeman, to write to her "Uncle Ed" with an unusual affection, given that she couldn't have spent much time with him. Many believed she was Edward Rulloff's daughter, alive and well and living in Pennsylvania. Rulloff never betrayed more than hints.

Not everyone believed Rulloff's confession to Freeman of Harriet's death. Other narratives—less crime of passion, more cold-blooded murder—had circulated for years, like the one he purportedly told his former defense attorney, Stephen Cushing, in which he chloroformed, smothered, then bled out his wife and child.

"It's a d—nd lie," Rulloff said. "I never told Cushing anything of the kind . . . He was no lawyer; he was a fool and a humbug, generally full of whiskey and gasconade." Of the murder of Frederick Merrick, Rulloff's confession stuck to the narrative that the clerk had used unwarranted force, that he was the beast, and had just enough chloroform in him "to make him crazy." From the moment Merrick woke up and grabbed his gun, Rulloff tried to calm him: "I went towards him, saying keep quiet, don't make any noise, and we wont [sic] hurt you." Rulloff stressed that he never meant to kill Merrick, only to keep the clerk from killing Jarvis.

> I took hold of Mirick [sic] and tried to pull him off but could do nothing with him. Jarvis said: "for God's sake take him off, he is killing me." I told him to let go or I would shoot him. He paid no heed to it. I fired one shot over his head. I did not intend to hit him. I was still in hopes he would let go. Jarvis partially raised up when I fired, and said,

'don't hit me.' Mirick forced him back again, and at the same moment *I fired a second shot and Mirick fell forward upon his face over Jarvis.*

Meanwhile, defense counsel George Becker was hard at work on the appeal process. In February, standing up once more against Peter Hopkins, Becker brought forth his argument to the supreme court in Albany that the burglars were, in fact, victims of the unwonted violence of the clerks. He lost. The judges upheld the guilty verdict. Becker persisted, asking judge after judge for writs of error, detailing missteps in the trial process, including the use of the photograph of the dead men, and attempting to get a new trial for his client. He argued the case once more in the Court of Appeals, and once more, the verdict was upheld. Rulloff's death sentence was now to be carried out on May 15.

Commutation was the next possible path away from the gallows, but only, Becker told Rulloff, if he were considered insane. Rulloff didn't want to be considered insane. He asked Freeman, "Ham, wont [sic] the Governor let me live to finish my book on Philology?" Freeman told him he didn't think he should be hanged, but only because he believed him to be insane. Still, at Rulloff's behest, Becker and Freeman brought scholars in to meet with him in the hope their good opinion would slow his fate.

Rulloff told Ham that if the governor would spare him long enough to finish his manuscript, "my mission on earth is performed; when my great book on philology is completed, and placed before the world, I shall be ready to die, and I don't care a d—m then how soon."

His book—his raison d'être—had gotten him into trouble by being the justification for all manner of criminal acts; his book, he still believed, would get him out of it.

Rulloff took language out of God's wheelhouse. He claimed that while God may have given man the raw materials to create language—for example, the ability to speak—it was man who created language. It was an unusual, though not original, viewpoint in nineteenth-century philology. Rulloff believed that all languages were derived from one ancient language and that their movements could be tracked across the globe. A more nuanced version of this is the basis of much linguistics today. The specifics of his theory were far wilder, though.

Rulloff believed that the original ancient language had been conceived and perfected all at once by a class of priests in secret. Encoded within all languages, he claimed, is the original secret method the priests developed that, once understood, would facilitate both the learning of languages and the comprehension of deep linguistic structures. Rulloff believed it would revolutionize and democratize language study.

To a man living on the edges of society, largely in poverty, and without the sanction of the academy, this must have been an attractive notion. With the method he'd uncovered, anybody could learn Greek or Latin or French. The problem was that the method was largely incomprehensible. He spent countless hours creating tortuous etymologies and made twisting claims about how words were related to one another that were difficult to follow and seemingly arbitrary. The roots of words, he maintained, were incorruptible, but certain consonants were interchangeable. In an interview with Oliver Dyer, a sympathetic reporter with a cosmopolitan readership in the *Sun*, Rulloff tried to give a clear example:

> It is a principle in the formation of a philosophical language that things which are opposites in meaning, are named from the same roots, in which the elements are reversed. Take the words stir and rest for example, the meanings of which are opposites. In stir, the root is composed of s, t, r; in rest these are reversed—r, s, t. Things relatively large and small are also named from the same roots. But it is impossible to illustrate this subject in a proper manner in an interview like this.

Even he couldn't find the words to explain it. Still, Rulloff was able to impress some scholars. When Richard H. Mather, a professor of Latin and German at Amherst College, visited him in prison, Rulloff invited him to test him on ancient texts of Mather's choice. He recited from memory a Socratic dialogue and excerpts from the *Iliad* and the plays of Sophocles. More surprising to Mather was Rulloff's analysis of the texts, which exhibited "such subtlety and discrimination and elegance as to show that his critical study of these nicer points was even more remarkable than his powers of memory . . . ." In writing up the interview, Mather didn't comment on Rulloff's theory, thinking it too complex for general readers, but he was struck by the condemned man's seeming indifference to his plight:

> He sat there in his chains, just sentenced by the highest Court to die on the gallows, and without a word, or

apparently a thought, for his doom, he argued and plead [sic] for his favorite theory, as though he were wrestling for his life.

Others were less impressed. The ten scholars Freeman and Becker had been able to scare up to visit Rulloff disagreed with his theory and refused to sign the petition to the governor he proffered. Another professor, George Sawyer, wrote up a visit he made to Rulloff in the *Journal of Insanity*. He dismissed Rulloff's performance with Mather as a deception: probably the man was just quoting the few things he'd learned by rote. When questioned on fundamental classic texts and translation, Sawyer found Rulloff silent and singularly unremarkable. His knowledge was "fragmentary and ill-assorted"; his theory's method was "fanciful" at best. Any portions of it that intrigued, he thought, were "borrowed" from a renowned philologist, Dr. Kraitsir. This was no genius; nor was he, in Sawyer's opinion, crazy. He was a con man. Rulloff, he claimed, was "a medical quack, a legal quack, a mechanical quack . . . , a photographic quack, a burglarious quack, a philological quack." Interestingly, vis-à-vis his medical career, Rulloff admitted to Ham Freeman that he felt himself "an empiric." What did he mean by "empiric?" Freeman asked. "Why, d—n it, a fraud!"

Worst of all, though, to Sawyer, Rulloff was "a moral monster." Sawyer fell into the camp of those who saw all of Rulloff's claims to scholarship as a con, a misdirection from his true and thoroughly criminal nature.

Another camp, represented by the founder and editor of the *New-York Tribune*, Horace Greeley, felt Rulloff was insane, and philology was the cause. In an editorial for the *Trib*, Greeley wrote, "His mind has dwelt so fixedly upon this absorbing theme that the usual morbid condition consequent upon too powerful and continued tension has resulted, and the man has gone mad." Further, Greeley boldly claimed, "He murdered the shopkeeper in the interest of philology." Rulloff himself, while he might have claimed a monomania for philological theory, would never accept a diagnosis of insanity.

One journalist of the day, who would go on to have the kind of glory and immortality Rulloff could only dream of, wrote a letter to the editor of the *New-York Tribune* in which he decried the coming sacrifice of "one of the most marvelous of intellects that any age has produced" and suggested an alternative:

> If a life be offered up on the gallows to atone for the murder Rulloff did, will that suffice? If so, give me the proofs, for in all earnestness and truth I aver that in such a case I will instantly bring forward a man who, in the interests of learning and science, will take Rulloff's crime upon himself, and submit to be hanged in Rulloff's place . . . .

April 29, 1871.
    SAMUEL LANGHORNE

This was Mark Twain, in the days before *Huck Finn* or *A Connecticut Yankee*. He was doing what he did best, writing with his pen nicely sharpened with satire. Unsurprisingly, no one stepped forward to slip their neck into a noose. Twain was playing the provocateur, hoping to get people talking about the possibility of commuting Rulloff's sentence. "The last paragraph (as magnificently absurd as it is)," he wrote in an accompanying note to the *Tribune*'s Whitelaw Reid, "is what I depend on to start the *talk* at every breakfast table in the land." Twain, though not a death penalty abolitionist, certainly had doubts about its application in some cases. On the eve of the publication of his book *Roughing It*, Twain wrote—and quickly thought better of—a dedication thought to be to Rulloff.

To the Late Cain

This Book is Dedicated:

Not on account of respect for his memory, for it merits little respect; not on account of sympathy with him, for his bloody deed placed him without the pale of sympathy, strictly speaking: but out of a mere humane commiseration for him in that it was his misfortune to live in a dark age that knew not the beneficent "Insanity Plea."

Rulloff's execution date was closing in. With just a week to go, George Becker was desperate. He paid a visit to Governor Hoffman in Albany and begged for the appointment of a lunacy commission.

The commission visited Rulloff's cell on May 10. Dr. John P. Gray of the Utica Lunatic Asylum and Dr. S. Oakley Vanderpool, an Albany doctor, were the whole of the commission, not counting Dwight King, the secretary they brought along. Rulloff met them with a disavowal: "Gentlemen, this is no work of mine. I don't pretend to be either insane or an idiot."

Rulloff was asking for more time to finish his book; the only way he would get more time is if the Commission deemed him insane. But if the merits of his book didn't, as he still hoped, save him; he'd rather die than be thought insane, for who would credit the theory of a mad man? A tidy catch-22.

Drs. Gray and Vanderpool questioned Rulloff on his theory and on such random things as to whether he thought Shakespeare had actually authored all the plays and poems thought to be his. Presumably there was some method to their questions, but the effect was to make Rulloff "show off how smart he was." With a determination to report him sane, the commissioners left, and with them his last best hope of a reprieve from the noose.

17

The trains into Binghamton on May 17 of 1871 were packed with country people eager to see the end of Rulloff. There was an air of festivity to the town; hotels and guest houses were at full capacity. Harriet Schutt's brothers Ephraim and Aaron were in attendance. They asked to see Rulloff, hoping to get some truth out of him as to the whereabouts of Harriet's body. He refused. "Not by a d—d sight."

Ham Freeman made one last ditch effort to plead with the governor for clemency. The telegram he sent arrived that night.

"Rulloff cannot be saved. All efforts will prove useless. I thank God I have done my duty as I understand it, and regardless of the consequences."

A second telegram arrived with official word that the governor would not intervene. That night also saw the arrival of George Sawyer's scathing report on his and Dr. Andrews' visit with Rulloff the previous Saturday. Rulloff's response was simply that they had only spent two hours with him, and it was impossible to explain his theory in such an abbreviated time.

He had made no plans for what would happen to his remains postmortem, right up to the night before the execution. When the sheriff asked, Rulloff said he "didn't care a damn what became of it." It was only at the very last minute that Rulloff decided there was likely to be considerable interest in his body after his death. He rushed to instruct that his brother be contacted to collect his remains. He was suddenly suspicious both of what might be done with his body and of people writing books that distorted his life story. That last night, he destroyed all the papers he'd been working on in his cell and lashed out at his allies. He was ungracious to his unfailingly faithful lawyer, George Becker; he denounced his friends and those "who had any trace of him" so that, in Ham Freeman's opinion, "the world should always remain in ignorance of his black crimes."

In line with his disavowal of the divine generally, Rulloff refused the presence of priests and ministers in the days before his execution. When a Roman Catholic priest approached him with a crucifix in his hand, Rulloff told him, "Take away that damned thing."

The press was in a frenzy to get to him, feeding the appetite for every detail of the killer's last days. They competed and mocked each other in print. Characteristically, Rulloff refused to talk about the case or his crimes, willing only to discuss science and his "linguistic labors." He told one reporter that he trusted his brother would publish his "great work" and "see to it that the result of my life is not lost to the world that rejects me in my hour of need."

Later, as the clock moved inexorably toward the dawn of his execution day, his watchman asked if he had ever "given a true history" of his life. Edward Rulloff replied that the history of his life would be told in his book.

Rulloff didn't sleep his last night alive. In case he decided to try to kill himself, three guards were set to watch him; his kerosene lamp was replaced with a candle. Certainly, suicide was something he'd talked about before with Ham Freeman:

> He had requested me to provide him with a lancet, and with fifteen grains of *sulphate of morphia* . . . in case his counsel were not successful in saving his life . . . He had several plans for me to give it to him. One was, to procure the lancet, take off the handle and place the blade in a book; the other was to put the morphia into one of two capsules.

Rulloff was awake to watch the daybreak and hear the cocks crow. He "asked facetiously what the rooster had to crow for at that unseasonable hour." He joked with his captors and a journalist and showed them trivial mathematical puzzles, which seemed to amaze them. The sheriff's parlor clock struck five. Rulloff startled. "How now—what was the hour, four?"

One of his guards asked if he'd killed Burrows. Rulloff said no; Jarvis did it and it was "all Merrick's fault." He reenacted the skirmish at Halberts store, demonstrating all the actors' positions, ignoring the impossibility of Jarvis having shot Merrick in the back of the head when he was bent over in Merrick's grip. Afterward, he fell to reading his books.

The hour tolled. "What o'clock is that, Thomas?" Six, his guard told him. "Ha! time is growing shorter!" His shackles now gone, he paced his cell, beads of sweat on his forehead.

He alternated between reading a dictionary (which, the reporter noted, was upside down) and conversing with his guards. When one asked for his autograph, Rulloff gave him a religious prison pamphlet he'd never had any use for and a copy of some of his shorthand. Calmer, he sat down to look through *Fox's Book of Martyrs*, lingering over the engravings of hangings.

As morning wore on, he received his last visitors: Sheriff Root of Tompkins County—hoping to learn the fate of Harriet and Priscilla—and George Becker, his attorney. The former, as every hopeful had before him (except Freeman), went away disappointed, the latter, Rulloff apologized to for his previous ingratitude.

He was anxious for the arrival of his brother, but when Becker showed him a delayed note he'd received from Rulloffson, it became clear he wasn't coming. Becker promised to do his best to carry out Rulloff's wishes that his remains be safe from desecration.

Rulloff didn't accept any food that morning but slowly sipped at a mug of coffee. At 9:00 a.m., when he was brought his execution garb to change into, he seemed to be back in control. He combed his hair carefully in front of a mirror, adjusted his frock coat, and tried to put on his boots, but the shackles had swelled his feet. He lay on the bed with his feet in the air for a few minutes to bring the swelling down. He took great care with his dress, maybe aware of the crowds awaiting him. And the crowds outside were huge, numbering in the thousands by most accounts, and included many women and children. It was hard, with such numbers, to get a clear view of events, but no one seemed to mind. The case was so famous and Rulloff such a strange and paradoxical character that people wanted to be in Binghamton on May 18 just to say they'd been there. One man, though, climbed up a ladder to the flimsy roof of a house so he could see Rulloff go to the gallows.

At 10:00 a.m. Rulloff asked Becker the time: "Ah, we have an hour more of it." And he ran his fingers down Becker's watch chain and darted his hand into his vest pocket, "as though in search of some means of ridding himself of life."

Ham Freeman showed up at 10:30 a.m., straight from his trip to New York City, where he'd made his final appeal to the governor. Freeman was overcome. "Stand firm, Ham; do not give way; you feel much more affected than I do," Rulloff told him. He shook hands with Freeman and kissed him. Freeman later mused, "I sometimes think that the reason why he embraced me on the morning of his execution was so that I could slip a capsule, containing poison, from my mouth into his."

By some accounts, Rulloff then pushed Ham Freeman away, apparently disappointed. No poison would save him now.

18

Judicial hangings come in four varieties: suspension hanging, the short drop, the standard drop, and the long drop. Rulloff would be hung by none of these.

By the middle of the nineteenth century, the intersection of science and ethics had stirred a movement to minimize the pain of execution. The Binghamton prison authorities decided to use a more modern method of hanging, fast becoming the standard in the state: the "upright jerker." Instead of a trapdoor through which the condemned would fall, a system of weights and pulleys would jerk him into the air. Ideally, the neck would snap, and death would come quickly and without strangulation. In practice, more often than not, the neck didn't break—and death came slowly, torturously. The counterweight had to be just right to offset the weight of the body. Too much weight, the prisoner would fly into the air, potentially decapitating him; too little, he would dangle, slowly asphyxiating.

The counterweight they hung in Binghamton on May 18 was 200 lb. to Rulloff's estimated 175.

At 11:15 a.m., a deputy rang a bell in the prison.

The sheriff placed the noose loosely around Rulloff's neck and pinioned his arms to his side above the elbow. As they were about to proceed out of the holding cell, Rulloff stopped.

"Boys, I must shake hands with you all up here, for I'll do nothing of the sort downstairs." They all shook his hand.

"You won't have any clergymen bellowing down there, nor prayers, nor any of that damned bosh, will you Mr. Sheriff?"

"No, sir," said the sheriff, and the group walked down the stairs, through the crowd of journalists and official guests in the prison yard to the gallows. Rulloff put his hands in his pockets.

The crowd all removed their hats, respect due to the dying—even if he was a killer—as Rulloff was positioned on his mark, and his knees and ankles bound. A deputy took ten minutes to read Rulloff his death warrant. Rulloff's hands stayed in his pockets.

The sheriff asked if he had anything to say before his sentence was carried out.

"Nothing at all."

The sheriff told him he had twenty-six minutes left to say his piece. Rulloff clenched his lips. A minute passed. "I cannot stand still!" he said, and went silent again.

The sheriff had not expected this reserve. While he consulted with his deputies, Rulloff turned to one of his guards. "I wish they would hurry this thing up."

The sheriff asked him if it was his desire that they proceed immediately.

Rulloff nodded.

Still, the sheriff hesitated. He asked again if Rulloff wished no delay.

Rulloff nodded.

At last, a deputy pulled a white cap down over the condemned man's face. The sheriff gave the signal.

The rope jerked Rulloff four and a half feet into the air above the limit of the rope. His right hand flew out of his pocket. As he fell back down, his hand fumbled for his pocket and slipped itself back in—one last nonchalant gesture of defiance.

Some newspapers reported that death was instantaneous. It actually took at least fifteen minutes for his pulse to fully stop. At twenty-three minutes, the doctors on hand declared Rulloff dead. Ten minutes later, they lowered the body into a coffin. The cause of death, they said, was a broken neck, but Rulloff's death was much more excruciating than that. The noose had strangled him slowly, but he had none of the usual signs of strangulation—the bulging eyes, the livid skin. On the contrary, he looked peaceful under the white hood.

Edward Rulloff's brother didn't come to collect his body and never had Rulloff's masterwork on philology published. But the last chapter of Edward Rulloff's story didn't end on the gallows that spring day. Just as he'd feared, his body was an artifact of keen interest to more than a few people.

Shortly after he'd been declared dead, two men from an Ithaca "art gallery" owned by Jefferson Beardsley made a "very satisfactory plaster cast of Rulloff's face and head"—a death mask. The gallerist no doubt saw money to be made from such an exhibit.

Sheriff Martin bowed to the public's rather macabre interest and let the body be displayed in an open coffin in front of the Binghamton jail. Thousands of people thronged to it, before Ham Freeman called the whole thing a "horrid exhibition" to George Becker, who had the sheriff move the body back into the jail.

Becker, as per Rulloff's wishes, was responsible for his remains until Rulof Rulloffson should come to claim them. The lawyer didn't wait long. The day after the hanging, Becker struck a deal with Dr. George Burr, a professor at the Geneva Medical College and the father of Dr. Daniel Burr, who'd testified at Rulloff's trial.

GEO. BECKER, ESQ.:—For the privelage [sic] of making

certain anatomical examinations and experiments upon the body of Rulloff, I will, after making such examinations decently inter his remains in a lot which I own in the old cemetery grounds.

May 19th, 1871.

GEORGE BURR.

Burr really only wanted his head. In studying the anatomy of Rulloff's head and brain, he hoped to crack the mystery of the nature of evil. Less than a day and a half after the execution, the Burrs—father and son—sawed the head off Rulloff's body and set about making meticulous measurements. It took them so long to saw through the cranium to get to Rulloff's brain, they began to think the head was "all skull." That night, the town sexton picked up the rest of the body and delivered it to the cemetery, where it was buried. No sooner had night fallen, though, than a group of medical students dug up the grave in quest of Rulloff's head. They were, of course, too late. They wouldn't be the last to try.

Newspaper illustration of medical students digging up Rulloff's body

By the end of the year, George Burr had presented his findings to the Medico-Legal Society in New York City and published them in an illustrated volume that also chronicled Rulloff's life in sensational detail. What he found in Rulloff's anatomy that contradicted theories of criminality he countered with other "findings" that supported it.

There was no doubt that Rulloff's head was large, his skull thick and his brain enormous. It weighed fifty-nine ounces. Albert Einstein's brain only weighed forty-three. Rulloff's was a few ounces shy of the heaviest brain ever recorded—that of the early nineteenth-century naturalist Baron Cuvier, which came in at around sixty-four ounces. Did this make Rulloff a genius?

Burr used other measurements to dispute it: the cerebrum, the presumed seat of intellect, he found, was smaller than the other, "brute," parts of the brain. The theory at the time that criminals were more "animal" than human, that there was a "criminal type," was, in Burr's estimation, borne out by his studies of Rulloff's brain.

Phrenologists agreed. A popular theory holding that the nature of a person could be detected by their physiognomy and the contours of the head, phrenology found an irresistible subject in Rulloff. Rulloff probably considered himself a phrenologist, having written at least two papers and possibly having lectured on the subject. But he would have come to a very different conclusion on the meaning of the size and shape of his head. Far from seeing genius, phrenologists published distorted descriptions of Rulloff's features and concluded that they marked a monster. For if Burr and the phrenologists had found more genius than criminal lurking in the head and brain tissue of Edward Rulloff, they might also have had to reckon with Mark Twain's lament that it was tragic to sacrifice such an intellect, when an insanity plea might have saved it.

In the end, George Burr didn't keep up his end of the bargain. Edward Rulloff's body was discovered many years later buried not in the promised plot but in the potter's field section of the cemetery, among the poor and unclaimed.

But Rulloff's brain just kept moving—first to Hobart College, then, under the keen stewardship of Dr. Burt Green Wilder, to Cornell University. Wilder himself, convinced that there was something to learn about evil in the structure and chemistry of the brain, established a formidable brain collection still housed at Cornell. It was Rulloff's dearest wish that he be remembered as a scholar, a leading intellectual light. In short, he wanted to be remembered for his brain.

Though Wilder's collection has deteriorated over the decades, eight jars still sit in a display case in Cornell's Department of Psychology, in each a human brain. Fourth from the left—and slightly greener than the others—is the brain of a murderer.

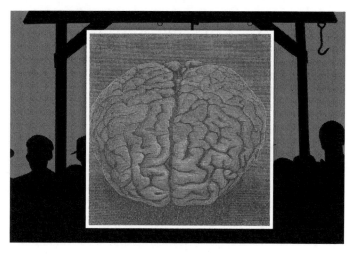

Illustration of Rulloff's Brain

A Word From C.J. March

Thank you for reading *Killer Genius*. If you have thoughts on this book or suggestions for other true crime accounts, please let us know at cjmarch@deadtruecrime.com. We love hearing from readers. You're why we write.

Sign up for our mailing list to learn about new Dead True Crime books and to read and listen to a free, exclusive story: www.deadtruecrime.com/ebook.

If you're interested in reading more about Edward Rulloff, check out the bibliography at the end of the book.

Other Dead True Crime Books

Sacrificial Axe
Voodoo Cult Slayings in the Deep South

The "Axe-man" came in the night. No one heard him come. No locks could keep him out. In the morning, whole families lay slaughtered in their beds, a riot of blood corrupting the room. Town by town, terror gripped the black communities of Louisiana and East Texas, as men, women, and children fell to the killer's ax. The police were powerless to stop it. Was it simply a homicidal maniac on the loose, or was a deeper evil afoot? Could one person perpetrate over forty atrocities? Was the serial killer even a man? People whispered voodoo, and white newspapers in the Jim Crow era South fanned the hysteria. As the police slowly unraveled the mystery, they were stunned by the bizarre truth of the "Axe-man."

Get Sacrificial Axe

Ghoul of Grays Harbor: Murder and Mayhem in the Pacific Northwest

Sailors trusted him with their money and their lives. That was a mistake. The lucky ones woke up with headaches in the holds of ships headed to China. The others never took another breath.

Billy Gohl robbed, 'shanghaied,' and killed sailors across the Pacific Northwest. Grays Harbor in Aberdeen, Washington was so full of bodies that newspapers dubbed it a 'floaters fleet.' His trapdoor of death was famous. In his time, Gohl murdered over 100 people, making him one of the most prolific serial killers in American history.

Get Ghoul of Grays Harbor

Poison Widow

Arsenic Murders in the Jazz Age

First, she predicts your death. Then, you die. Usually, writhing in pain. Is she a fortune teller, or something much, much darker? Nobody tells the police, not for a long time, because, well, nobody in Chicago's Little Warsaw wants to cross Tillie Klimek. The body count racks up as Jazz Age Chicago's most notorious female poisoner takes down husband after husband, and some other relatives while she's at it. Few, it seems, can resist Tillie's cooking. But is this Mrs. Bluebeard working alone? Or is she part of a bigger, more diabolical "poison trust"? And can Chicago's Finest get to her before her latest husband, already mortally ill, dies? *Poison Widow* is a true-crime aficionado's feast, arsenic-laced and stuffed with tasty noir morsels.

Get Poison Widow

Murderer's Gulch
Carnage in the Catskills

Don't turn your back on her. Don't even blink. She may be crazy, but Lizzie Halliday is strong, she moves fast, and she's a stone cold killer. When famed journalist Nellie Bly interviews the woman the New York Times called "The Worst Woman on Earth," she has no idea how easy it would be for Lizzie Halliday to make Bly her next victim. In the peaceful Catskills in upstate New York, Halliday dispatches husbands, neighbors and peddlers by fire, poisoning and gunshot. The bloody death count at the Halliday farm earns it the name, "Murderer's Gulch." But even after she's arrested and committed to an insane asylum, Lizzie Halliday will kill again.

Get Murderer's Gulch

Coming Soon

Exit Row
Mass Murder in the Canadian Sky

A clear day. An experienced pilot. A routine flight. An obsessive love-triangle. What could go wrong? When a mysterious package follows J. Albert Guay's wife on board Flight 108, calamity is just a few ticks of the clock away. How far will a man go for his adulterous passion?

Cannibal Cowboy
Murder and Man-Eating on the American Frontier

Gold Rush and gunfights, scalping and saloons, the Old West had a reputation to uphold. But even the rough and tumble frontier wasn't ready for the likes of the Kentucky Cannibal. Mountain man and gunfighter Boone Helm would do anything to survive, right down to eating his enemies. Or his friends.

Blood Trade
Slaughter on the Underground Railroad

Nothing could be worse than slavery. Unless it was Patty Cannon hunting you down. A gang of thugs at her command, the woman infamous for her blood-thirst and brutality murdered free blacks and fugitive slaves alike for decades. Working her illegal slave trade in what became known as the Reverse Underground Railroad, Cannon's grisly tactics still have the power to chill centuries later.

About the Author

C.J. March is the alter ego of three true crime enthusiasts who wanted to write the kind of juicy noir histories they like to read. Between them they have: 2 MFAs, 3 arrests, 4 folk albums, 73 years of therapy, 1 stint working for "the artist formerly known as" which ended in a shoving match, 40 years of writing, 30 years of design, 3 dogs, and 1 overnight in a cell with a murderer.

Bibliography

"The American Traupmann." *New York Herald*, January 25, 1871.

Bailey, Richard W. *Rogue Scholar: The Sinister Life and Celebrated Death of Edward H. Rulloff.* Ann Arbor: University of Michigan Press, 2003.

Banner, Stuart. *The Death Penalty: An American History.* Cambridge: Harvard University Press, 2003.

Bradbury, Tara. "Treatment at Her Majesty's Penitentiary in St. John's Called 'Unfair and Sickening.'" *Telegram* (St. John's, Newfoundland), March 16, 2018.

Breslaw, Elaine G. *Lotions, Potions, Pills and Magic: Healthcare in Early America.* New York: NYU Press, 2012.

Burr, George. *Medico-Legal Notes on the Case of Edward Rulloff with Observations upon and Measurements of His Cranium, Brain, etc.* New York: D. Appleton and Company, 1871.

Comfort, G. F. (letter to the editor). *New York Times*, May 23, 1871.

Crapsey, Edward. *The Man of Two Lives: Being an Authentic History of Edward Howard Rulloff Philologist and Murderer*. New York: American News Company, 1871.

"Edward Rulloff, Philologist and Murderer." *New York Times*, January 12, 1871.

"Execution of James Stephens." *New York Times*, February 4, 1860.

"The Execution of Rulloff." *Ithaca Journal*, May 25, 1871.

Freeman, E. H. *Edward H. Rulloff: The Veil of Secrecy*

Removed. 1871. Reprint on demand, Lowood Press, 2011.

"The Hanging of Rulloff." *New York Sun*, May 19, 1871.

Life, Trial and Execution of Edward H. Rulloff. Philadelphia: Barclay and Co., 1871.

MacCarald, Clara. "Archeology Helps Tell the Story of the Cayuga Nation." *Ithaca Times*, September 14, 2014.

Mason, Frank R. "The American Silk Industry and the Tariff." *American Economic Association Quarterly*, 3rd ser., 11, no. 4 (December 1910).

"The Missing Daughter of the Murderer Rulloff—An Improbable Story." *Broome Republican* (Binghamton), January 24, 1871. Reprint, *New York Times*, January 26, 1871.

"A Modern Eugene Aram." *New York Sun*, January 25, 1871.

"The Murderer Rulloff: His Alleged Confession." *Utica Herald*, January 13, 1871. Reprint, *New York Times*, January 14, 1871.

New York State Court of Oyer and Terminer (Broome County). *Life, Trial and Execution of Edward H. Rulloff*. Miami: HardPress, 2017.

"Notes." *Nation,* February 23, 1871.

Parker, Amasa J., ed., "The People v. Edward H. Rulloff." *Reports of Decisions in Criminal Cases Made at Term, at Chambers, and in the Courts of Oyer and Terminer of the State of New-York*. Albany: W. C. Little & Company, 1858.

"Rulloff." *New York Times,* January 12, 1871.

"Rulloff Doomed." *New York Times*, April 6, 1871.

"Rulloff Hanged." *New-York Tribune*, May 19, 1871.

"Rulloff; Report and Conclusions of Drs. Gray and Vanderpool." *New York Times*, May 13, 1871.

"Rulloff; The Sentence of the Law Executed upon the Murderer." *New York Times*, May 19, 1871.

"The Rulloff Trial." *New York Times*, January 7, 1871.

"The Rulloff Trial." *New York Times*, January 8, 1871.

"The Rulloff Trial." *New York Times*, January 9, 1871.

"The Rulloff Trial." *New York Times*, January 11, 1871.

"The Rulloff Trial." *New York Times*, January 12, 1871.

"Rulloff's Brain." *New York Times*, May 24, 1871.

Sawyer, George C. "Edward H. Rulloff." *American Journal of Insanity* 28, (1871–1872).

"A Substitute for Rulloff." *New York Daily Tribune*, May 3, 1871.

Thurston, Thomas. "Hearsay of the Sun: Photography, Identity, and the Law of Evidence in Nineteenth-Century American Courts." *American Quarterly: Hypertext Studies in American Scholarship* (1996). http://chnm.gmu.edu/aq/photos/index.htm.

Tomes, Nancy J. "American Attitudes toward the Germ Theory of Disease: Phyllis Allen Richmond Revisited." *Journal of the History of Medicine* 52 (January 1997).

"The Trial of Rulloff." *Ithaca Journal*, January 10, 1871.

"The Trial of Rulloff for Murder." *Ithaca Journal*, January 17, 1871.

Twain, Mark. *The Letters of Mark Twain, volume 4, 1870–1871*. Edited by Victor Fischer, Michael B. Frank, and Lin Salamo. Berkeley: University of California Press, 1995.

Young, Jay. "Infrastructure: Mass Transit in 19th- and 20-Century Urban America." *Oxford Research Encyclopedias: American History* (March 2015). http://oxfordre.com/americanhistory/view/10.1093/acrefore/9780199329175.001.0001/acrefore-9780199329175-e-28.

Image Credits

CHAPTER 1
Illustration of the "Drowned Burglars." From Crapsey, *The Man of Two Lives*.

CHAPTER 2
Newspaper illustration of Rulloff assaulting his wife with a pestle. From *Life, Trial and Execution of Edward H. Rulloff*.

CHAPTER 5
Portrait of Rulloff. From Crapsey, *The Man of Two Lives*.

CHAPTER 9
Newspaper illustration of the crime. From *Life, Trial and Execution of Edward H. Rulloff*.

CHAPTER 11
Portrait of Frederick Merrick. From Freeman, *Edward H. Rulloff: The Veil of Secrecy Removed*.

CHAPTER 19
Newspaper illustration of medical students digging up Rulloff's body. From *Life, Trial and Execution of Edward H. Rulloff*.

Illustration of Rulloff's brain. From Burr, *Medico-legal Notes on the Case of Edward H. Rulloff*.

KILLER GENIUS. Copyright © 2019. Slingshot Books. All rights reserved. No part of this book may be used or reproduced in any manner whatsoever without written permission except in case of brief quotations embodied in critical articles or reviews. For information address Slingshot Books, LLC. 2628 30th Avenue South, Minneapolis, MN 55406.

Slingshot Books
Minneapolis

www.slingshotbooks.com

Made in the USA
Middletown, DE
26 July 2019